INFINITE WORTH

Discovering Your Identity In Christ In A Rapidly Changing World

JOSEPH L. MILTON

Table of Contents

PART 2: GOD REVEALED

PART 3: APPLICATION

PART 4: IMPLICATIONS

INTRODUCTION

Disruption

Wow, the world is being disrupted! Rapid advancements in technology are transforming our lives in unimaginable ways. I cannot believe I have a self-driving car. We have more information at our fingertips than history's greatest museums and libraries combined. At the same time, we can create our own online world to align with our worldview and craft carefully managed online personas. Yet, despite being more connected than ever, many of us feel increasingly isolated.

I remember using the Encyclopedia Britannica to write my school reports. Now, we can simply prompt ChatGPT or even use it to help author a book, which I did. I thought I was mobile with a beeper; all I had to do was find a payphone to call you back on your landline. Now, not only do we carry phones with reliable service, but these devices also grant us access to the internet, text messaging, GPS, social media, audiobooks, music, movies, photos with professional-quality cameras, and more memory and processing power than supercomputers that once filled entire rooms. What a time to be alive!

We are living in the next Industrial Revolution, called Industry 4.0, a fusion of technologies blurring the lines between the physical, digital, and biological spheres that have facilitated an unprecedented rate of change and confusion. This unique time in history comes with new opportunities and risks. As technology reshapes our world and redefines how we interact, it is crucial to anchor ourselves in something unchanging. Discovering our identity in Christ provides this steadfast foundation needed to thrive amid the shifting sands of modern life.

In this increasing chaos, Christians have a unique opportunity to become the steady presence the world needs for this new era. People who are willing to serve, love, and stand on enduring values. Yet there are common personal barriers that limit our ability to truly serve and love others, such as the desire for approval, validation, control, and security. These barriers manifest themselves when we hesitate to reach out to others for fear of rejection, when we prioritize our comfort over serving those in need, or when we seek control in an uncontrollable world. These barriers must be removed and replaced with an anchor if we are to thrive amid increased disruption. We will explore these together in later chapters.

As we grapple with these personal barriers, societal trends further complicate our ability to connect authentically. It is becoming harder and harder to determine what is true and what is misinformation. Imagine what it will be like in the near future as deep fakes get better and better. Reality itself will become distorted. This disruption is leading to division and dehumanization of others. Many people now live in echo chambers of news, social media, and political affiliations that destroy empathy and connection. This isolation supports the "Cancel Culture" that cuts off people who do not align with a particular viewpoint.

How can Christians build meaningful relationships in this environment? How is it possible to speak truth in love, serve sacrificially, engage graciously and not follow the loudest voices or latest trends? These are some of the questions we will be exploring together. Here is a quick overview of what will be covered:

Part 1 – Identity and Purpose in Christ
We will discover what *identity* and *purpose* are, why we are constantly searching for them, and how God alone fills our longing. Many of our challenges stem from a misalignment of *identity* and *purpose*. As the world around us is disrupted, those resting in Christ have an anchor that holds and roots that keep them grounded in ultimate truth.

Part 2 – God Revealed
We will delve into the ways God has been revealed in the resurrection of Jesus, biblical prophecy, and God's character in the Gospel.

Part 3 – Application
We will explore how Christ's work is applied in our lives here and now.

Part 4 – Implication
We will look forward to the promises of a new creation, a new humanity, and the glorious future that awaits us.

As we renew our hearts and minds to understand who God is and who He created us to be, we can reflect His glory to those around us in this unique time in history. There are practical steps we can take together to understand who we are and why we are here.

Are you ready to discover who you were always meant to be?

PART 1

Identity and Purpose in Christ

CHAPTER 1

Chaos Versus Design

A *re we here by chance or is there a purpose to this life?*
If you are reading this book, my assumption is you are either a Christian or at least open to exploring what you believe and why. We live in a world that is moving increasingly toward a foundational belief that we are here by chance and there is no such thing as truth. We can be pulled in this direction if we are not intentionally cultivating our worldview. If we do not take the time to understand the implications of chaos versus design, we may choose the popular idea that we are here by chance, chaos. Chaos allows us to justify anything. What we believe about chaos versus design shapes how we see ourselves, how we handle life's hardships, and how we pursue our purpose.

I have wrestled with these questions, especially when life felt chaotic or when trying to weigh science and faith on my journey. As we prepare to dive into identity and purpose in the coming chapters, there is value in grounding ourselves on the foundation that there is a Creator. We are not merely atoms floating around by chance, chemical reactions without a soul or meaning. Let's explore these competing world views.

The Weight and Appeal of Chaos

For many in the world today, the idea that life is simply the product of random chance has a certain appeal. If everything is chaos—if we are just here by accident—then we get to define our purpose. We are free to create meaning, live as we want, and make our own path. It can feel liberating, like we are in complete control. But what happens when that freedom turns into uncertainty? What happens when things fall apart despite all our efforts?

I know that feeling all too well, the moments when nothing makes sense. You think you are in control, that your hard work and planning will bring order to your life, but then something happens that shatters that illusion. Maybe it is an unexpected loss, a diagnosis that changes everything, or the end of a relationship you thought would last forever. In those moments, when life feels random, it is easy to feel lost. If there is no deeper meaning, what is the point? If life is truly chaotic, then we must create meaning on our own, and that can be an overwhelming burden to carry.

French philosopher Albert Camus famously described life in a chaotic, meaningless universe as "absurd." He wrestled with the tension between our desire for purpose and the seeming indifference of the universe in *The Myth of Sisyphus* (1942), where he writes, "Man stands face to face with the irrational. He feels within him his longing for happiness and for reason. The absurd is born of this confrontation between the human need and the unreasonable silence of the world."

We try to build something meaningful, but deep down, we know it is fragile, temporary. It is like trying to build a sandcastle at the edge of the sea no matter how carefully you craft it, the waves will eventually wash it away. Have you ever felt the weight of knowing that no matter how hard you try, everything can be swept away in an instant?

The Futility of Life Without Design

Thousands of years ago, the writer of Ecclesiastes wrestled with this same feeling. He explored wisdom, pleasure, wealth, and hard work, only to conclude that, apart from God, everything felt empty. "Meaningless! Meaningless! says the Teacher. Utterly meaningless! Everything is meaningless" (Ecclesiastes 1:2, NIV[1]). This ancient cry echoes the frustration many of us feel when we chase after success, approval, or pleasure, only to find that they do not satisfy.

It is the feeling you get when you achieve something you have worked so hard for, but once the moment passes, you are left asking the question, *is this all there is?* It is the emptiness that comes when we have built our lives around things that fade; the writer of Ecclesiastes describes it repeatedly as "chasing after the wind" (Ecclesiastes 2:11)—trying to grasp something you cannot hold onto, but it always slips through your fingers.

The Real Implications of Chaos

For those who genuinely believe that life is chaotic and random, the implications are significant. Purpose is not something to discover, it is something they must create. However, creating your own purpose can feel like walking a tightrope without a net. Any sense of meaning you build is fragile because it depends entirely on you.

---

1. Scripture quotations are taken from the Holy Bible, New International Version throughout this book. NIV®. Copyright © 1973, 1978, 1984, 2011 by Biblica, Inc.® Used by permission. All rights reserved worldwide.

In a chaotic worldview, morality becomes relative if it exists at all. If there is no higher authority, no ultimate design, then what is right or wrong is something we construct ourselves. Morality shifts with culture, preferences, or circumstances. But deep down, we know that certain things, such as justice, love, and compassion, are not just human inventions. They speak to something deeper inside each of us. Those who believe that life is random struggle to understand why Christians feel so strongly about right and wrong because they have no reason to believe that right and wrong has already been determined.

And what about identity? If we are the product of random chance, then who we are is something we must construct. Our identity becomes tied to what we do, how we perform, or how others see us. But what happens when those things change? When we fail, when we are rejected, when life does not go as planned, does our identity crumble with it? An identity built on the hope that we measure up is fragile.

In a chaotic worldview, death is the final curtain. There is no afterlife, no eternal purpose, just the end. For some, that is comforting, but for many, it creates a sense of urgency, a need to grab as much pleasure and success as possible before time runs out. But even in the pursuit of pleasure, we often find ourselves coming up short. The writer of Ecclesiastes experienced this too: "I denied myself nothing my eyes desired; I refused my heart no pleasure . . . Yet when I surveyed all that my hands had done and what I had toiled to achieve, everything was meaningless, a chasing after the wind" (Ecclesiastes 2:10-11).

The Intention of Design

Christians believe there is a design, a purpose woven into the fabric of creation. The Bible begins with a declaration that sets the tone for everything else: "In the beginning, God created the heavens and the earth" (Genesis 1:1). This is not just an account of how things started; it is a statement that life was created with intention, purpose, and meaning. We are not the result of random chance. We are part of a story authored by the Creator who knows us intimately.

We see evidence of design all around us. Scientists have discovered that the universe is fine-tuned for life in ways that boggle the mind. If even one physical constant, like the force of gravity, were slightly different, life would not be possible. This precision points to intentionality. The world was not thrown together by accident; it was carefully crafted with purpose. As we move forward in the book, we will explore the profound implications of design.

SUMMARY OF KEY POINTS

- Chaos suggests that life is random, purposeless, and fragile, leaving us with the overwhelming task of creating our own meaning and identity.

- Ecclesiastes speaks to the futility of a life without God, where human efforts and pleasures feel empty and meaningless.

- In a chaotic worldview, identity, morality, and purpose are fragile and subjective. In a designed worldview, they are gifts we receive from a loving Creator.

REFLECTION QUESTIONS

1. Do you believe life is the result of chaos or design? How has this belief shaped your sense of purpose and identity?

2. How might your perspectives shift if you fully embrace the idea that your life was designed with purpose?

ACTION STEP

- Spend time reflecting on Ecclesiastes 1 and 2 and how it speaks to the feeling of meaninglessness without God. Then, turn to Genesis 1 and Psalm 139 and reflect on the concept of design and purpose. Consider how these passages challenge or affirm your understanding of your purpose and identity.

CHAPTER 2

Identity

We all have an internal call that we are meant for more, especially when we take the time to pull away from the temporal distractions. Deep down we have a longing to be fully known, loved, and accepted. In this time of disruption, distraction is easier than ever and uncertainly keeps us seeking more ways of escape. We often strive to fill this void, many times without even realizing it.

In today's rapidly changing world, we are constantly bombarded by images of what life 'should' look like. Social media feeds us a steady diet of perfectly curated moments—success stories, flawless bodies, and effortless achievements. We scroll, compare, and measure ourselves against these snapshots, hoping that if we can match up, we will finally feel like we belong. But the more we chase this illusion, the more we find ourselves asking, *why do I still feel empty?*

At the same time, and in stark contrast, our culture tells us to "be true to ourselves," to define who we are on our own terms. The world encourages us to create an identity based on our passions and the image we choose to present to others. It is a call to stand out, to be unique, to craft a version of ourselves that expresses our individuality. But what happens when the identity we have crafted starts to feel like a burden? When the version of ourselves that we present does not match the reality of who we are, it becomes exhausting to maintain the facade, and we are left wondering if we will ever be truly known. The anxiety increases as deep down we know that even though we desire to be fully known, loved and accepted that if the real us was exposed, we would be rejected.

In addition, our culture offers us false hope, asking us to turn to things less than what we were created for to seek significance, security, and value. As Tim Keller writes in *Counterfeit Gods: The Empty Promises of Money, Sex, and Power, and the Only Hope that Matters* (©2009, Dutton), we are offered false gods to worship that are not necessarily bad in themselves. Ancient false gods had names and temples and idols, but modern false gods might be good things like our work, relationships, money, or even the approval of others. But when we rely on them to define us, they inevitably let us down. The promotions, the praise, the perfect image all promise to fill the void, but instead, they leave us chasing after something that always slips through our fingers.

Matching the images that bombard us, being true to ourselves, and the worship of false gods can never truly satisfy. They may offer momentary fulfillment, but they always leave us wanting more. We were never meant to bear the weight of our identity. There is a reason why, even after reaching our goals, we still feel that restless longing. It is because we were made for something far greater.

The Bible calls us to discover that our ultimate value and identity is found in the *Imago Dei*, which literally means we are made in the image of God. This means that you and I have inherent worth, not because of what we do but because of who we were created by. This is not a value that fluctuates with our achievements or failures; it is a worth that is rooted in the One who made us. It is only when we discover this true identity that we find the freedom to stop striving and start living.

How do we let go of the false gods and distractions we cling to so tightly? This journey is not about quick fixes or easy answers. It is about confronting the reality of our brokenness by acknowledging the ways we have tried to build our identity on things that can never sustain us and discovering the grace that has been there all along waiting to meet us in our most vulnerable moments.

Jesus offers us a way forward. He says in Matthew 11:28-30, "Come to me, all you who are weary and burdened, and I will give you rest. Take my yoke upon you and learn from me, for I am gentle and humble in heart, and you will find rest for your souls. For my yoke is easy and my burden is light." This is not a promise of a life free from challenges but an invitation to find a rest that goes deeper than circumstances, a rest that comes from knowing you are loved and valued just as you are.

So, if you have felt exhausted by the relentless pursuit of worth, if you question why even your greatest successes still leave you wanting more, or if you carry a burden that feels too heavy to bear, this journey is for you. Together, we will confront the lie of hope in things that fail us and discover the deeper hope of what we were truly made for.

SUMMARY OF KEY POINTS

- We all sense a deeper calling and desire to be fully known, loved, and accepted.

- Our culture inundates us with ideals of success and images of perfection that leave us feeling empty.

- Simultaneously, we are told to "be true to ourselves," crafting an identity that can become burdensome if it does not reflect who we truly are.

- We often rely on "false gods" to find worth, but they inevitably let us down.

- Our identity and worth are found in the *Imago Dei*—being made in God's image, which means we have inherent value.

- Embracing our God-given identity frees us from striving and allows us to rest in Christ's love and acceptance.

REFLECTION QUESTIONS

1. In what areas of your life have you sought to define your worth through achievements, approval, or possessions?

2. How does understanding that you are created in God's image shift your perspective on your value and identity?

3. Where have you experienced the exhaustion of maintaining a false self-image, and what fears prevent you from embracing your true self?

ACTION STEPS

1. Write down the ways you have tried to find worth in external factors and note how they have fallen short.

2. Spend time reading and reflecting on Matthew 11:28–30. Consider memorizing it as a reminder that your rest and worth are found in Christ.

CHAPTER 3

Glorious Purpose

Why am I here?

It is a question that echoes in the depths of our souls, especially when we begin to wrestle with who we truly are—our identity. In the first chapter, we reviewed the idea that our identity is not something we have to earn or construct. it is a gift rooted in being made in the image of God. Although to fully grasp this, we need to go back to the very beginning, to the foundation of our story, and understand how we ended up so confused about who we are.

In the opening chapters of Genesis, we find a breathtaking account of creation. God spoke the universe into existence, crafting the heavens and the earth, the sun and the stars, the land, and the sea. However, His masterpiece was humanity. "So God created mankind in his own image, in the image of God he created them; male and female he created them" (Genesis 1:27). We were created without sin, reflecting God's character and glory. We walked with Him in the garden, enjoying unbroken fellowship and intimacy.

Our purpose was clear: to steward creation, to cultivate the earth, and to live in harmony with God and one another.

God gave Adam and Eve meaningful work, entrusting them with the care of His creation. Their identity was secure, they were His beloved children, made to reflect His image. There was no striving, no insecurity, no confusion about their worth or purpose. Everything they did flowed naturally from who they were in God's design.

Then something went terribly wrong. In Genesis 3, we read about the serpent's deception and the tragic choice that changed everything. Tempted by the promise of being "like God," Adam and Eve ate from the forbidden tree. In that moment, sin and death entered the world. Their perfect relationship with God was fractured, and shame replaced innocence. They hid from God, realizing their nakedness and vulnerability.

This act of disobedience did not just alter their circumstances, it disrupted their very identity. The *Imago Dei*, the image of God within them, was marred. They began to experience fear, shame, and a sense of separation from the One who had created them. The clarity of their purpose was clouded, and the harmony they once knew was replaced by discord.

The Apostle Paul reflects on this in Romans 5:12: "Therefore, just as sin entered the world through one man, and death through sin, and in this way death came to all people, because all sinned." This inheritance of sin affected all of humanity. We experience confusion, striving, and longing for something more because of this brokenness. Our understanding of who we are and why we exist has been distorted.

Nevertheless, the story does not end with our brokenness. God, in His infinite love and mercy, had a plan to restore what was lost. He did not abandon us in our confusion and sin. Instead, He pursued us, setting in motion a redemptive plan that would culminate in the life, death, and resurrection of Jesus Christ.

Romans 5:18-19 tells us, "Consequently, just as one trespass resulted in condemnation for all people, so also one righteous act resulted in justification and life for all people. For just as through the disobedience of the one man many were made sinners, so also through the obedience of the one man many will be made righteous."

Through faith in Jesus, our identity is restored. We are forgiven, redeemed, and brought back into right relationship with God. We become "co-heirs with Christ" (Romans 8:17), adopted into God's family. The Holy Spirit comes to dwell within us, guiding us, transforming us, and empowering us to live out our true purpose.

So why are we here?

If our identity is rooted in being made in God's image and restored through Christ, then our purpose is to reflect His glory in all we do. We are called to love God and love others (Matthew 22:37-39), to be ambassadors of reconciliation (2 Corinthians 5:18-20), and to make disciples of all nations (Matthew 28:19-20). Our purpose is not about achieving personal greatness but about participating in God's redemptive work in the world.

When we understand that our worth comes from who we are in Christ, we are freed from the pressure to prove ourselves. Our actions become a response to God's love rather than a means to earn it. We find joy in serving, giving, and living out the unique gifts and passions He has placed within us.

The Pursuit of Lesser Things

For years, I misunderstood this connection between identity and purpose. I believed that if I could achieve enough, accumulate enough, or earn enough approval, I would eventually fulfill my purpose. I poured my energy into reaching goals, building my reputation, and proving my worth, convinced that purpose was something I had to create. Although each time I reached a milestone, the satisfaction was fleeting. It was as though every success was a faint echo of something greater that I could not quite grasp.

When we do not understand our identity, we end up chasing lesser things, hoping they will give us a sense of purpose. We strive for promotions, relationships, accolades, and material possessions, believing they will fill the void. However, these pursuits, while they may offer temporary fulfillment, always fall short. They were never meant to carry the weight of our purpose because they are not tied to who we truly are.

Think about it. How many times have you achieved something you thought would bring you lasting fulfillment only to find yourself feeling emptier. That is because our purpose was never meant to be defined by what we do but by who we are in a relationship with, the One who created us.

The Loki Analogy: Chasing Illusions of Control and Purpose

This struggle reminds me of the Marvel series *Loki*. Loki, the God of Mischief, is convinced that he is destined for a "glorious purpose: "to rule, to be in control, and to shape his own destiny. But his idea of purpose is entirely rooted in proving himself, in being seen as powerful and significant. He believes that if he can just seize enough power, he will finally be who he is meant to be.

As the series unfolds, Loki discovers that there are forces far greater than him, the Timekeepers, who have been orchestrating events all along. Suddenly, the "glorious purpose" he believed in unravels, revealing itself to be an illusion. This revelation shatters Loki's sense of identity and purpose, leaving him to question, *If I am not in control, then who am I?*

Loki's journey reflects our own struggle with purpose and control. When we root our purpose in what we can achieve or control, we end up chasing illusions. We think that if we can just attain the right job, relationship, or level of success, we will finally feel significant. But like Loki, we find ourselves asking, *is this really what I was meant for?*

The Contrast: God's Sovereign and Loving Purpose

This is where our story takes a different path. Unlike the Time-keepers, who represent an indifferent form of control, God's purpose for us is full of love, grace, and compassion. While Loki is left feeling powerless in the face of forces beyond his control, we find that our lives are held by a God who knows us intimately and desires good things for us.

In Jeremiah 29:11, God declares, "'For I know the plans I have for you,' declares the Lord, 'plans to prosper you and not to harm you, plans to give you hope and a future." This verse doesn't mean trusting God is going to give us whatever we want. Then he would just be another way to chase the lesser gods we talked about earlier. God's purpose for us is not about control or manipulation. It is about inviting us into a relationship where we can discover the fullness of who we were created to be.

The Freedom of Walking in God's Purpose

Walking in God's purpose frees us from the relentless pressure to prove ourselves. It liberates us from the lie that we need to be perfect, successful, or admired to be worthy. Instead, we are invited to rest in the knowledge that we are already loved, already chosen, and already significant in the eyes of God. This is a radical shift from the world's definition of purpose, and it is one that brings true freedom.

When we stop chasing after lesser things and start walking in the purpose God has for us, we find that life becomes more meaningful, more fulfilling, and more aligned with who we were created to be. Our purpose is not something we have to create; it is something we step into as we align ourselves with God's heart.

Purpose Unlocked Through Surrender

One of the most profound aspects of walking in our true purpose is the realization that it is unlocked through surrender. Not striving but letting go of the need to control every outcome and trusting that God's plan for our lives is far more glorious than anything we could imagine. We do not need to have it all figured out; we simply must be willing to follow where God leads.

When I began to surrender my plans, ambitions, and need for validation, I discovered a deeper sense of purpose than I had ever known. I found that my purpose was not just about accomplishing remarkable things but about being faithful in the small things. It was not about gaining recognition but about making a difference in the lives of those around me. This shift in perspective allowed me to see that my purpose was woven into the fabric of everyday life, not just the big moments.

Walking Out Who We Are

Our purpose flows naturally from our identity. Because we are created in God's image, we are called to reflect His character in our words, actions, and relationships. We are designed to be vessels of His love, channels of His grace, and bearers of His truth. When we embrace this calling, we begin to experience the fullness of life that God intended for us.

We are not made to strive to create a purpose, but we are made to walk in the one God has already prepared for us. We need the understanding that our identity, as His beloved children, gives us the confidence to step into our unique calling without fear or hesitation. We do not have to be perfect; we just need to be willing to trust. As we take each step, trusting in His guidance, we discover that our lives are part of a much larger story; one that is infinitely more beautiful than anything we could have written ourselves.

SUMMARY OF KEY POINTS

- Our purpose flows naturally from our identity. Being made in the image of God is foundational to understanding our worth and identity. It forms the foundation for discovering our true purpose.

- Without a clear understanding of our identity, we often pursue achievements, approval, and material success, hoping they will bring fulfillment. These "lesser things" may offer temporary satisfaction but leave us empty, as they were never meant to define our purpose.

- Like Loki in the Marvel series, who seeks a "glorious purpose" through control, we too can chase illusions of significance based on power or success. True purpose, however, is not found in what we control but in surrendering to God's design.

- In contrast to Loki's experience of an indifferent power dictating his life, we find reassurance in God's loving and sovereign purpose.

- Embracing God's purpose liberates us from the relentless pressure to prove ourselves, shifting our perspective from achievement to acceptance in God's love. In this freedom, we realize we are already loved, significant, and chosen by God.

- Our true purpose is revealed through surrender, not control, as we allow God to lead us. This surrender frees us from self-centered ambitions, revealing a deeper purpose rooted in faithfulness to God in both small and significant moments.

- When we embrace our identity in Christ, our purpose unfolds in our daily actions, relationships, and words. By reflecting God's love and grace, we live out our calling, contributing to His larger, beautiful story beyond what we could accomplish alone.

REFLECTION QUESTIONS

1. How have you been pursuing purpose in lesser things, and how has that pursuit left you feeling empty?

2. What would it look like for you to start living out the purpose God has already designed for you, rather than striving to create your own?

3. How does understanding your identity in Christ give you the confidence to walk in your God-given purpose?

ACTION STEPS

• Take time this week to reflect on how your gifts, passions, and experiences can be used to serve others and glorify God.

• Pray and ask God to reveal the areas where you have been striving for purpose in your own strength and invite Him to guide you in walking out His purpose for your life.

• Choose one practical way to live out your purpose today, whether it is encouraging someone, using your talents to bless others, or stepping out in faith in an area where God is calling you.

PART 2

God Revealed

CHAPTER 4

God Revealed in the Resurrection of Christ

We previously described the feeling that something is missing, even when everything is going well, that restless feeling that there is still something more no matter what you achieve or experience. Deep inside each of us there is a longing, a God-shaped hole, that nothing in this world can truly fill.

We are left searching, always looking for something deeper, something more permanent. This endless cycle of searching leads us to a big question: Has this Creator, this something more, been revealed?

When we look at the vastness of the universe or the intricate beauty of life, we cannot help but wonder if there is a Designer behind it all. Religions and philosophies throughout history have attempted to answer that question, each offering different paths toward meaning. Christianity alone presents something radical, that God came down to us rather than us working our way up to God.

In Christianity, God is not distant or unreachable. He became one of us, stepping into human history in the person of Jesus Christ, living the life we could not live, and offering us redemption through His death and resurrection.

Christianity's Unique Claim

Imagine hearing someone claim to be God. Not just a prophet, not just a wise teacher, but God in human form. It would have sounded audacious, blasphemous, right? Yet that is exactly what Jesus claimed.

Jesus did not simply come to point us toward God. He claimed to *be* the way. He boldly declared, "I am the way, the truth, and the life" (John 14:6). He did not say He *knew* the way; He said He *was* the way. His statements were not just metaphors or philosophical musings. They were claims of divine authority. "Before Abraham was born, I am" (John 8:58). He identified Himself with the eternal God of the Old Testament. He did not just teach about God's kingdom; He claimed to be its King, saying, "I and the Father are one" (John 10:30).

These were not small claims. They were radical, and they ultimately got Him crucified. However, what sets Jesus apart from any other religious figures is not just what He said, it is what He did. Jesus backed up His claims with His life, His death, and His resurrection. This is the foundation of Christianity: the belief that God Himself entered our world to rescue us.

The Necessity of the Resurrection

At the heart of the Christian faith is the resurrection of Jesus. Without it, everything falls apart. As Paul puts it in 1 Corinthians

15:14, "And if Christ has not been raised, our preaching is useless and so is your faith."

The resurrection is not just a validation of Jesus' claims. It is the foundation of Christian hope. It tells us that death does not have the final word, that Jesus' victory over sin and death is also our victory. Imagine that for a moment. If Jesus really rose from the dead, then there is hope beyond death. There is power greater than anything we can imagine. The hope is not just for Him; the promise of the resurrection is for us, too.

Historical Evidence and Implications

The resurrection of Jesus is not just a comforting idea or a theological concept. It is a historical event that carries profound implications for the Christian faith and for how we understand life, death, and eternity. The evidence surrounding the resurrection points us to the reality of this miraculous event, giving us a firm foundation for our faith. Let's walk through some key pieces of evidence and consider what they mean for us today.

These are quick high-level summaries, and I recommend taking time for deeper research to learn more about the evidence with resources such as *The Case for Christ* by Lee Strobel.

The Empty Tomb

Imagine being one of the women who went to Jesus' tomb that first Easter morning. You are carrying spices, preparing to anoint the body of your friend and teacher, overwhelmed with grief. You expect to find a sealed tomb, but instead, the stone is rolled away, the tomb is empty, and angels appear, declaring that Jesus has risen. The emotions in that moment—fear, confusion, awe—must have been overwhelming.

What is remarkable about this account is that women were the first witnesses. In the cultural context of the first century, the testimony of women was not considered reliable in legal or religious matters. If the early Christians were fabricating the story, they would not have chosen women as the first to witness and report such an extraordinary event. Even if women were the first witnesses, the "better" way to tell the story at the time would have been to skip to any men who were there. The fact that the Gospels record women as the primary witnesses to the resurrection suggests a deep commitment to telling the truth, no matter how culturally inconvenient or unlikely it seemed.

Think about it. The most important event in human history is first entrusted to those who, by societal standards, would not be believed. This is a testament not only to the integrity of the resurrection accounts but also to the nature of God's kingdom, a kingdom that often operates contrary to human expectations and values. Jesus' resurrection defied cultural norms and demonstrated that God's ways are not our ways (Isaiah 55:8-9).

Post-Resurrection Appearances

The empty tomb alone would raise questions, but the resurrection is further confirmed by Jesus' appearances to His followers after His death. According to 1 Corinthians 15:6, Jesus appeared to over five hundred people at once, as well as to His disciples, and to Paul himself. These were not fleeting visions or vague spiritual experiences. These were physical, bodily appearances of the risen Christ.

Consider that these witnesses were real people who could be questioned and challenged. Paul names them in his letter, essentially inviting anyone with doubts to go and speak to those who had seen Jesus alive. If these appearances were fabricated, it would have been easy for the contemporaries of Paul to discredit them. Yet, no such evidence exists, and many of these witnesses went on to face persecution and death for their belief in the risen Christ. People do not willingly die for what they know to be a lie. The fact that these men and women were willing to give their lives for the truth of the resurrection is compelling evidence that they had encountered the living Jesus.

The Transformation of the Disciples

Before the resurrection, Jesus' disciples were frightened, hiding behind locked doors, confused and unsure about what had happened. They had followed Jesus, believing He was the Messiah, but His crucifixion shattered their hopes. Peter, one of Jesus' closest disciples, even denied knowing Him out of fear for his life.

Then after the resurrection, something changed. These same disciples, who had been terrified and disillusioned, became bold proclaimers of the Gospel. They traveled throughout the Roman Empire, declaring that Jesus had risen from the dead and offering eternal life to those who would believe. What caused this dramatic transformation? It was not a vague spiritual belief or a comforting metaphor. It was the reality that they had seen Jesus alive, risen from the dead.

Peter, who had denied Jesus three times, would go on to preach boldly at Pentecost, declaring the truth of the resurrection to thousands. Thomas, who famously doubted, would proclaim, "My Lord and my God!" after seeing the resurrected Jesus with his own eyes (John 20:28). The fear and uncertainty of the disciples were replaced by a fearless conviction that Jesus was alive, and that conviction fueled the explosive growth of the early church.

The Growth of the Early Church

Despite facing intense persecution, the early church grew at an unprecedented rate. The message of the resurrection spread like wildfire, not because it was a comforting idea, but because it was an undeniable reality. The disciples did not proclaim Jesus as a moral teacher or a martyr for a noble cause. They declared Him as the risen Lord, the conqueror of death.

In the Roman Empire, Christians were persecuted, imprisoned, and even killed for their faith. Yet, instead of fading away, the church continued to grow. Why? Because the resurrection of Jesus had fundamentally changed everything. The early Christians were willing to endure hardship, suffering, and even death because they knew that death had been defeated. The resurrection was not just a doctrine to believe. It was the foundation of their hope and the power behind their mission.

Historian N.T. Wright has argued that the growth of the early church is unexplainable apart from the resurrection. There is no historical precedent for a movement like Christianity to emerge and thrive under such oppressive conditions unless something truly extraordinary had happened. That extraordinary event was the resurrection.

Imagine Being There

Now, imagine walking with the disciples after the resurrection. You have seen Jesus crucified, buried, and now, alive again. You are sitting with Him, hearing His voice, seeing the scars in His hands, and understanding that everything He promised has come true. The One who was dead, is now alive, and nothing will ever be the same.

How would that change your life? How would it reshape the way you see your struggles, your purpose, your future? The resurrection is an invitation to see beyond the limitations of this world, to live with the confidence that death does not have the final word. The same power that raised Jesus from the dead is now at work in us, giving us new life and a hope that cannot be shaken.

Christ's Divinity and Victory

The resurrection of Christ validates His victory over death and His claims to not just be a created Savior, but God in the flesh, revealing a truth that sets Christianity apart from any other world religion: the Trinity. It is the fullest revelation of who God is to us and His eternal character. I was surprised the first time I realized that the word "Trinity" is not in the Bible, yet the concept is written all over the pages, foreshadowed throughout, and made clear on this side of the resurrection.

The Trinity: God the Father, God the Son, and God the Holy Spirit

Understanding the nature of God as revealed in the Bible brings us face-to-face with one of the greatest mysteries of the Christian faith, the concept of one God existing in three persons—Father, Son, and Holy Spirit. It is foundational to Christianity, even though it is impossible to fully grasp since God is beyond the capabilities of our minds. While each person of the Trinity shares the same divine essence, they also have distinct roles that together reveal the fullness of God's nature and His relationship with us. Before we jump into the details, I want to remind you that the Trinity is above our full comprehension. It took the early church a lot of time and effort to understand the nature of God and the incarnation of Jesus by the means of several councils and the development of creeds. I encourage you to keep studying and exploring for a fuller picture and how we have the understanding we have today. Let's explore the unique role of each person within the Trinity.

God the Father: The Creator and Sovereign Sustainer

Imagine the universe, vast and intricate, each star placed with purpose, each life formed with care. God the Father is the ultimate source of everything. He spoke the world into existence, setting the universe in motion with His powerful word. Genesis 1:1 reminds us, "In the beginning, God created the heavens and the earth," highlighting God as the Creator of all things. The Father is the architect of creation, the one from whom all life flows.

Yet God the Father is not only the Creator. He is also the Sovereign Sustainer. Romans 11:36 reminds us, "For from him and through him and for him are all things. To him be the glory forever! Amen." The Father holds all things together through His will, continually guiding, providing, and caring for His creation. He didn't simply set the world in motion and walk away; He is actively involved in every detail, sustaining life, and maintaining His creation.

As our Father, God is personal and relational. He knows each of us intimately, calling us His children (1 John 3:1). The God who created the stars and governs the universe also knows the number of hairs on your head (Luke 12:7). This is the level of care and attention He gives to each one of us—far from being distant, He is a loving Father who desires to walk with us and be known by us.

God the Son: Jesus—The Visible Image and Sustainer of All Creation

Jesus Christ, the Son of God, is not only the Savior who died for our sins but also the one through whom and for whom all things were created. Colossians 1:16-17 powerfully affirms this truth: "For in him all things were created: things in heaven and on earth, visible and invisible, whether thrones or powers or rulers or authorities; all things have been created through him and for him. He is before all things, and in him all things hold together." Jesus is called the visible image of the invisible God, and through Him, everything is created and sustained.

When we look at Jesus, we see the heart of God up close. In Christ, God stepped into our world, taking on human flesh to live among us. This is most clearly revealed in John 1:14, where we read, "The Word became flesh and made his dwelling among us." This comes right after John explained the "Word" was in the beginning, and was with God, and was God. Once we see that the

"Word" (or Logos, in Greek) refers to Jesus, we can see one of the clearest statements in Scripture of the one God existing in more than one person. Then, as the Word becomes flesh, Jesus lived the perfect, sinless life we could not, showing humility, compassion, and love in every action. He touched the untouchable, healed the broken, and spoke life into those forgotten by society.

Jesus also clearly claimed to be one with the Father. In John 10:30, He declares, "I and the Father are one." This claim of oneness led to opposition from religious leaders because they understood it as a claim to divinity. Additionally, in John 14:9, Jesus said, "Anyone who has seen me has seen the Father," emphasizing His role as the visible manifestation of God.

One of the most powerful demonstrations of Christ's divinity is His authority to forgive sins. In Mark 2:5-7, when a paralyzed man was brought to Jesus, instead of immediately healing him, Jesus declared, "Son, your sins are forgiven." The religious leaders were shocked and thought to themselves, "Who can forgive sins but God alone?" By forgiving the man's sins, Jesus was making a direct claim to divinity. He then healed the man, showing His authority not just over sickness, but over sin as well, affirming His divine power.

Jesus also made another remarkable claim about His identity in John 8:58, saying, "Very truly I tell you, before Abraham was, I am!" This statement is significant because "I AM" is the name God used for Himself when speaking to Moses in Exodus 3:14 ("I AM WHO I AM"). By using this phrase, Jesus was directly identifying Himself with Yahweh, the God of Israel, which is why the religious leaders sought to stone Him for blasphemy (John 8:59).

Throughout the Gospels, Jesus repeatedly demonstrated His divine authority in ways only God could, including calming storms (Mark 4:39), raising the dead (John 11:43-44), and casting out demons (Matthew 12:22). His most significant declaration of His divine nature, however, is through His resurrection, confirming His victory over sin and death.

God the Holy Spirit: The Indwelling Presence of God

After Jesus ascended into heaven, He promised that we would not be left alone. He sent the Holy Spirit, the third person of the Trinity, to be our Comforter, Counselor, and Guide (John 14:26). The Holy Spirit is God's presence with us now, actively working in the lives of believers to bring about transformation and empower us to live according to God's purposes.

The Holy Spirit is not an impersonal force but a personal, relational presence of God within us. He works in our hearts to reveal the truth of Scripture, convicts us of sin, and strengthens us when we are weak. He helps us understand God's will and enables us to walk in step with His plans. It is the Holy Spirit who produces the fruit of the Spirit in our lives: love, joy, peace, patience, kindness, goodness, faithfulness, gentleness, and self-control (Galatians 5:22-23).

In Matthew 28:19 Jesus commands His disciples to baptize "in the name of the Father and of the Son and of the Holy Spirit." The singular "name" (rather than plural "names") and the equal listing of Father, Son, and Holy Spirit together strongly suggest the Spirit's full divinity, co-equal with the other persons of the Trinity. In 1 Corinthians 2:10–11 Paul notes that the Spirit searches "the deep things of God," knowing God's thoughts. Omniscience, knowing even the depths of God's own mind, is a divine attribute. This ability places the Holy Spirit in the realm of deity, as no created being can fully comprehend God.

What is truly remarkable is that the same Spirit who raised Jesus from the dead now lives in us (Romans 8:11). This means that God's power is not only for the future resurrection but is also available to us today as we seek to live out our calling in Christ. The Spirit equips us for ministry, helps us overcome sin, and reminds us daily that we are children of God (Romans 8:16).

Summary of the Trinity

The Father, Son, and Holy Spirit are distinct persons, yet they exist in perfect unity as the one true God. The Father is the Creator and Sovereign Sustainer, overseeing all things. The Son, Jesus, is the visible image of the invisible God, through whom all things were created and are sustained. The Holy Spirit is the indwelling presence of God, empowering and guiding believers in their daily walk with Him.

Together, the Trinity reveals the fullness of God's love, grace, and power, inviting us into a relationship with Him that transforms every aspect of our lives.

The Invitation to Know the Creator

So where does all of this leave us? If the resurrection is real—if God has truly revealed Himself through Jesus and continues to work in us through the Holy Spirit—then we are faced with a choice. The God who created the universe, who became human in Jesus, and who now dwells within us through the Holy Spirit, invites us into a relationship with Him.

This is not about following religious rules or trying to earn God's favor. It is about knowing the God who created you, who loves you deeply, and who has a purpose for your life. The God-shaped hole inside you can only be filled by Him. That longing you feel, the one that no achievement, no relationship, no amount of success can satisfy is the voice of your Creator, calling you to something deeper.

The Hope of the Resurrection

The resurrection is not just a historical event. It is the foundation of our hope. Because of the resurrection, we know that death does not have the final word. Pain and suffering are not the end of the story. We are loved by a God who was willing to step into our brokenness, take our place on the cross, and rise again in victory.

This changes everything.

When we look at the world, it is easy to feel overwhelmed by the chaos, the suffering, the brokenness. Nevertheless, the resurrection reminds us that this world is not all there is. There is a greater story being written. One that ends with redemption, restoration, and resurrection for all who trust in Christ.

The hope of the resurrection is that we, too, will one day be raised to new life. We will be given new bodies, free from pain and suffering, and we will live forever in the presence of God. This hope gives us the strength to endure the struggles of this life, knowing that something far greater is waiting for us.

SUMMARY OF KEY POINTS

- Christianity claims that God became human in Jesus Christ, revealing Himself through His life, death, and resurrection.

- The Trinity—Father, Son, and Holy Spirit—shows us a God who is relational, loving, and deeply involved in His creation.

- The resurrection of Jesus is the foundation of Christian faith, offering hope and new life based on historical evidence.

REFLECTION QUESTIONS

1. What does the resurrection mean to you? How does it shape your view of life and death?

2. How do you understand God's relational nature through the Trinity?

ACTION STEP

- Take time this week to reflect on the resurrection. Read John 19-20 and imagine yourself walking through those events. What does it reveal about God's love for you? How does it change the way you see your own life?

CHAPTER 5

God Revealed in the Bible

We touched on this last chapter, but I want us to take a moment to see that the Bible is not a collection of random books or stories. The story of redemption is woven into the very fabric of creation, and even before the moment of humanity's fall, God was working his plan for redemption, inviting us into a story that spans all of time. God's love and sovereignty are seen not only in promises but also in the intricate ways He fulfills them, proving that His care for us is not passive or distant but intimately active. Each sign, prophecy, and foreshadow lead us toward a Savior who was the ultimate plan of redemption all along.

The Fulfillment of All Scripture

One of the most beautiful affirmations of this truth comes from Jesus Himself. After His resurrection, on the road to Emmaus, He encounters two of His disciples who are disheartened and confused by the recent events. Unrecognized by them, Jesus begins to walk alongside and asks what troubles them. As they express their despair, Jesus responds not with immediate revelation of His identity but by taking them through the Scriptures.

"And beginning with Moses and all the Prophets, he explained to them what was said in all the Scriptures concerning himself" (Luke 24:27). He shows them that what they saw as a shocking story of defeat was a long-foretold story of victory.

Later, when He appears to His disciples, He says, "This is what I told you while I was still with you: Everything must be fulfilled that is written about me in the Law of Moses, the Prophets, and the Psalms" (Luke 24:44).

These moments are profoundly beautiful because they show Jesus as the thread woven through every part of Scripture. He does not dismiss the Old Testament as obsolete; instead, He reveals that it has always been a testimony about Him. The laws, the prophecies, the poetry all whisper His name. Jesus illuminates the following Scriptures, turning what was once opaque into a glorious revelation of God's redemptive plan.

Bruising the Serpent's Head: The First Gospel Whisper

In Genesis 3:15, when humanity first stumbled into sin, God's response is striking. Rather than immediate judgment, He gives a promise to overcome evil. Addressing the serpent, God says that one day a descendant of Eve will "crush your head, and you will strike his heel." This passage, known as the protoevangelium, is the first mention of the Gospel, the good news that God will heal the world. Here, the story of salvation is set into motion. Though veiled in mystery, it foretells a day when the enemy's power will be broken, and sin's grip shattered by a Savior who will suffer yet overcome.

After Christ, we see this passage clearly as pointing to Jesus in a way the original audience never could. He is the "seed" of the woman who, through His crucifixion (the bruising of His heel), would defeat Satan (crushing the serpent's head). This momentary suffering led to ultimate victory over sin and death, showing a God who promises victory from the very start. He did not leave humanity to languish in sin; He demonstrated His love through the long arc of history.

A Bronze Serpent Lifted Up: Healing by Faith

As the people of Israel journeyed through the wilderness, their doubt and disobedience brought consequences, and a plague of venomous snakes entered their camp. Desperate, the people cried out to Moses, and God instructed him to make a bronze serpent and lift it high on a pole. Whoever looked upon this serpent would be healed.

This scene in Numbers 21 might seem peculiar, yet Jesus Himself later references it as a sign of His own death. "Just as Moses lifted up the serpent in the wilderness, so must the Son of Man be lifted up, that everyone who believes may have eternal life in him" (John 3:14-15). The parallel is beautiful and profound. In the wilderness, Israel had only to look in faith at the bronze serpent to be healed from the deadly venom. On the cross, Jesus, lifted up, became the source of our healing, our remedy for the deadly venom of sin. The simplicity of looking in faith underscores that salvation is a gift we simply receive—God has done the work. God could have just healed the afflicted or removed the snakes, but instead he gave us an image in real history of the coming redeemer.

Through this sign, God shows us His power over all things, including our brokenness. Jesus bore our sin, took the curse upon Himself, and became our source of life and healing. God's love meets us in our most desperate need just as it met the Israelites in theirs.

Abraham's Dilemma

Step back for a moment into one of the most pivotal moments in the Old Testament. Imagine being Abraham in the story we hear in Genesis 22. You have waited years for God's promise of a son, and finally, you have Isaac, the child through whom God said He would build an entire nation. Now, God asks you to sacrifice him.

Can you picture it? Walking up the mountain with Isaac, the wood for the sacrifice on your son's back, your heart heavy with dread. What was going through Abraham's mind? The confusion, the heartache, the trust. And yet, even in this unimaginable moment, Abraham believed that God had a plan. At the last moment, God provided a ram, a substitute sacrifice, which spared Isaac's life.

This story points forward to the ultimate act of God's love. Just as Isaac carried the wood up the mountain, Jesus carried His cross to Calvary. Although this time, there was no substitute. Jesus was the sacrifice. God provided His only Son as the Lamb who takes away the sin of the world. God asked Abraham to be willing to sacrifice his son for God, but God actually did sacrifice his son for humanity.

The Passover Lamb

Now picture the scene in Exodus 12. The Israelites are in Egypt, enslaved and crying out for deliverance. God instructs them to take a spotless lamb, sacrifice it, and place its blood on the doorposts of their homes. That night, the angel of death passes over every house marked by the blood, sparing the lives of their first-born sons.

Can you imagine the weight of that moment? Knowing that the blood of the lamb was the only thing standing between your family and death. This powerful image points us to Jesus, the ultimate Passover Lamb. His blood does not just save us from physical death. It saves us from eternal separation from God.

As Paul writes in 1 Corinthians 5:7, "For Christ, our Passover lamb, has been sacrificed." Jesus' death and resurrection were not random events. They were part of God's plan from the beginning, foretold in stories like the Passover.

Psalms and Prophets: A Symphony of Promises

In the Psalms, we see God revealing glimpses of a suffering Messiah centuries before Jesus walked the earth. Psalm 22 paints an eerily specific picture of crucifixion long before it existed as a method of execution. The psalmist writes, "They pierce my hands and my feet . . . they divide my clothes among them and cast lots for my garment" (Psalm 22:16-18). These exact details play out in Jesus' crucifixion proving that every moment of His life, every act of His suffering, was written into God's plan.

Psalm 34:20's prophecy that "not one of his bones will be broken" was fulfilled in the unique nature of Jesus' death. Though it was customary for the legs of the crucified to be broken to hasten death, Jesus had already died, fulfilling this prophecy (John 19:33-36). Isaiah 53 provides a similar foretelling: "He was pierced for our transgressions, crushed for our iniquities; the punishment that brought us peace was upon him, and by his wounds we are healed." This prophecy reveals a Messiah who would not only bear physical suffering but would take on the full weight of our sins.

The Triumphal Entry

The book of Zechariah also foretold the way the Messiah would enter Jerusalem: "See, your king comes to you . . . lowly and riding on a donkey" (Zechariah 9:9). Jesus' entry into Jerusalem, celebrated on Palm Sunday, matches this description (Matthew 21:1-11). This act, both humble and powerful, displayed Jesus as the King who came not to conquer with force but to save with love.

The Depth of God's Love and Sovereignty

Each prophecy, some written hundreds and others over a thousand years before Jesus' birth, finds its fulfillment in meticulous detail in His life, death, and resurrection. These fulfillments showcase not only God's foreknowledge but His active, unwavering involvement in the story of humanity. He wove together the threads of time, people, and events to reveal His love through His Son.

God's plan was never an afterthought. Jesus' life was not a reaction to human failure, but the culmination of a promise given in Eden. The beauty of this story is that God's sovereignty is not cold or mechanical—it is saturated with love. He orchestrated history not just to prove His power but to show His relentless pursuit of us. This pursuit tells us that God is both mighty and tender; He moves empires and comforts the brokenhearted.

SUMMARY OF KEY POINTS

- The Old Testament is filled with prophecies that find precise fulfillment in the life, death, and resurrection of Jesus, showcasing God's sovereignty and love.

- Jesus Himself affirmed that all Scriptures point to Him, revealing that the entire Bible tells one cohesive story of redemption.

- These fulfilled prophecies demonstrate that God's Word is trustworthy and reveal His deep, active love for humanity.

REFLECTION QUESTIONS

1. Which prophecy about Jesus resonates most with you, and why?

2. How does knowing that Jesus Himself said all Scriptures point to Him change your perspective on the Old Testament?

3. In what ways can you seek Jesus throughout all of Scripture, and how might this deepen your relationship with Him?

4. How does seeing the specific fulfillment of prophecies change your understanding of God's involvement in your life?

5. What steps can you take to trust in God's sovereignty, knowing that He has a perfect plan?

ACTION STEP

- This week, read Genesis 1 to see the beginning of the redemption plan, and then read Luke 24:13-35 to reflect on how Jesus reveals Himself through all Scriptures.

CHAPTER 6

The Good News

The Gospel, or the "good news," is precisely that: a proclamation of what has been done for us, not what we must do. The heart of Christianity is the incredible message that salvation has been secured by Christ. When He hung on the cross, His last words were "It is finished" (John 19:30). This statement was a declaration that the debt of sin had been paid in full. He did not come simply to set an example, but to be a substitute for us, completing the work of salvation through His sacrifice alone.

In the Old Testament, priests were tasked with offering sacrifices for the people's sins day and night. But when Jesus, our perfect High Priest, offered Himself, He sat down at the right hand of the Father (Hebrews 10:12). His seated position symbolizes that His mission was accomplished, His once-for-all sacrifice was sufficient for all time, for you and for me.

Jesus lived the life we could never live, a perfect, sinless life. He took on human flesh, became like us, and then died the death we deserved. Not only did He remove our sins, but He gave us

His righteousness, allowing us to be called children of God (John 1:12). We are fully known, fully accepted, and fully loved not because of anything we have done but because of Christ's redeeming work on the cross. His grace is freely available to all who call upon His name. Let's review the impact and need for this grace.

Impact and Need of Grace

The Beauty of Grace in Les Misérables

In Victor Hugo's masterpiece *Les Misérables*, grace is a central theme vividly illustrated through the story of Jean Valjean. After spending nineteen years in prison for stealing a loaf of bread, Valjean is embittered and hardened. His life takes a profound turn when he is shown unexpected kindness by Bishop Myriel. After stealing the bishop's silver and being caught, the authorities bring Valjean back to the bishop. Instead of condemning him, the bishop forgives Valjean and even gives him more silver, saying, "You forgot these candlesticks." This extravagant act of grace, so undeserved and unexpected, transforms Valjean's life. The mercy he receives compels him to become a man of compassion and integrity.

This encounter mirrors the grace of God, which we receive through Christ. Just as the bishop's kindness reshaped Valjean's heart and future, God's grace transforms us. Grace is not earned; it is a gift completely unmerited and freely given. In *Les Misérables*, the power of grace is portrayed as life-changing, and this echoes the transformative power of God's grace in the Gospel.

The Need for Grace

To truly grasp the good news, we must first confront the reality of our need for grace. The Bible paints a clear picture of this grace. Romans 3:23 says, "For all have sinned and fall short of the glory of God." Sin, in its simplest form, is the act of missing the mark. It is a failure to live up to the perfection that God, as a holy and just Creator, requires. Due to sin, we are separated from Him. The consequences of that separation are severe: "For the wages of sin is death" (Romans 6:23, NIV). This is not just physical death but spiritual death, which is a total disconnection from God, the source of life.

Here is where the Gospel shines its brightest. While we were lost, while we were hopelessly cut off from God by our own choices and rebellion, God did not leave us to face the consequences alone. Instead, He extended His grace, a grace so profound that it changes everything. Romans 6:23 continues, ". . . but the gift of God is eternal life in Christ Jesus our Lord." Notice that shift. We go from wages (something we earn) to a gift (something freely given). This is the heart of grace.

Grace Defined

At its core, grace is the unmerited favor of God. It is receiving something we could never earn and certainly do not deserve. The Bible is filled with stories of God's grace toward people who failed and fell short. Whether it is the story of David, a man after God's own heart who committed adultery and murder, or Peter, who denied Jesus three times, grace is woven through Scripture as the great equalizer. No one is beyond the reach of God's grace, and no one can earn it.

Think about it: grace, by definition, must be a gift. If we could earn it, it would not be grace. Rather, it would be wages or payment. But Ephesians 2:8-9 tells us clearly, "For it is by grace you have been saved, through faith—and this is not from your-selves, it is the gift of God—not by works, so that no one can boast." We are not saved by our own efforts, our goodness, or our ability to live a righteous life. We are saved because of God's grace, period.

If you are like me, this knowledge is life giving. I know my failures. I know my weaknesses. I know I do not measure up and would need to hide or pretend if grace was based on my efforts.

The Bridge Between God and Humanity

Grace comes to us through the person of Jesus Christ. He is the bridge that connects our broken, sinful selves to a holy God. 1 Timothy 2:5 says, "For there is one God and one mediator between God and mankind, the man Christ Jesus." Jesus' life, death, and resurrection are the foundation of our faith. He lived a sinless life, fulfilling the law perfectly. Something we could never do on our own.

Jesus, being fully God and fully man, took the punishment that we deserved. On the cross, He bore the weight of our sins. Every lie, every act of rebellion, every selfish thought was all placed on Him. Isaiah 53:5 tells us, "But He was pierced for our transgressions, He was crushed for our iniquities; the punishment that brought us peace was on Him, and by His wounds we are healed." Jesus did not just suffer for the sins of the world in some abstract way; He suffered for your sins and mine, personally, and in doing so, He reconciled us to God.

However, the story does not end with His death. The resurrection of Jesus is the ultimate victory over sin and death. As 1 Corinthians 15:3-4 explains, "Christ died for our sins according to the Scriptures, that he was buried, that he was raised on the third day according to the Scriptures." Through His resurrection, Jesus conquered the grave, proving that sin's penalty had been paid in full, and that new life was possible for all who believe in Him.

His Grace Is Sufficient

We live in a culture that values performance. Whether it is success in our careers, achieving goals, or gaining approval from others, we are often measured by what we accomplish. But grace offers us something radically different. Grace says that our worth is not tied to what we do; it is tied to who God is and what He has done for us. Romans 5:8 tells us that "God demonstrates his own love for us in this: While we were still sinners, Christ died for us." God's love and grace are extended to us not because we earned them but because He chose to love us, even in our most broken state.

This is both freeing and humbling. On the one hand, we no longer must strive to prove our worth or earn God's favor. On the other hand, we are reminded that we could never deserve the grace we have been given. It is humbling to realize that all our efforts, no matter how well-intentioned, fall short. And yet, God's grace is sufficient.

Living in Grace

Understanding grace is one thing, but living in it is something else entirely. Grace should change the way we live, the way we interact with others, and the way we view ourselves. When we fully grasp the magnitude of God's grace, it frees us from the exhausting cycle of trying to prove ourselves.

Grace invites us to authenticity. We do not have to hide our failures or pretend we have it all together. We can be real with God and with others because we know that our identity is not based on what we do but on what Christ has done for us. This is the freedom that grace offers. It allows us to be vulnerable, knowing that we are loved and accepted, not because of our performance but because of God's love.

Grace also empowers us to extend that same love and grace to others. When we understand how much we have been forgiven, we are able to forgive. When we realize how undeserving we are of God's kindness, we can show kindness to those who do not deserve it. Grace flows from God to us, and then through us to the people around us.

The Mission of Jesus

Throughout His ministry, Jesus was clear about His mission, which was all about proclaiming and offering God's grace.

To Liberate: Jesus said, "The Spirit of the Lord is on me . . . He has sent me to proclaim freedom for the prisoners and recovery of sight for the blind" (Luke 4:18). Christ's mission was to free us from the bondage of sin and spiritual blindness, offering true freedom.

To Heal: Jesus came to heal our spiritual brokenness: "It is not the healthy who need a doctor, but the sick . . . I have not come to call the righteous, but sinners" (Matthew 9:12-13). His grace restores us from the inside out.

To Seek and Save the Lost: "For the Son of Man came to seek and to save the lost" (Luke 19:10). Jesus actively seeks those who are lost in their sins, offering them the grace of salvation.

To Give Life: Jesus promised, "I have come that they may have life, and have it to the full" (John 10:10). His grace not only saves us, but it gives us abundant life—rich in love, purpose, and joy.

To Serve and Give His Life as a Ransom: "The Son of Man came . . . to give his life as a ransom for many" (Mark 10:45). Jesus' ultimate act of grace was giving His life on the cross to pay for our sins.

The Call to Respond

The Gospel is a call to respond to God's grace. Jesus offers forgiveness, new life, and eternal hope to anyone who comes to Him. It is an open invitation to leave behind our old ways of striving and self-sufficiency and to accept the gift of salvation.

If you feel God drawing you to Him, now is the time to respond. You can surrender your life to Christ and accept His grace by praying a prayer like this:

"Dear God, I know that I am a sinner and cannot save myself. I have fallen short of Your glory, and I need Your forgiveness. I believe that Jesus Christ is Your Son, that He died on the cross for my sins, and that He rose again, conquering sin and death. I now place my faith in Jesus Christ alone for my salvation. I turn from my sin and surrender my life to You. Come into my heart and be the Lord of my life. Thank You for loving me, saving me, and giving me the gift of eternal life. In Jesus' name, Amen."

For those who already believe, this is a reminder of the incredible gift of grace you have received. Let it deepen your gratitude and inspire you to live more fully in the light of God's love. Share this good news with others, so they, too, can experience the transforming power of grace.

Embracing a New Identity

One of the most profound truths in the Christian faith is the reality that, in Christ, we are given a completely new identity. It is not just a change in how we feel about ourselves or a new set of beliefs we hold; it is a fundamental transformation of who we are. No longer are we defined by our past failures, our sins, or the labels the world places on us. Instead, we are called children of God, heirs to His promises, and members of His family. This is not something we earn or achieve through effort or merit. It is a gift, a gift of grace that we receive through faith in Christ.

Living in this new identity is a daily journey. This is a journey which requires us to constantly remind ourselves of who we are in Christ, especially when the world tries to tell us otherwise. We can rest in the truth that we are loved, forgiven, and empowered, regardless of how we feel or what our circumstances may look like. We can embrace the freedom that comes from knowing our worth is secure in Jesus.

As we walk in this new identity, we begin to see how God's grace transforms not only our relationship with Him but also our relationships with others. We are free to love, free to forgive, free to serve, and free to live authentically. This is the gift of grace. It changes everything.

Loved and Accepted

We are deeply loved by God, in a way that is almost incomprehensible. It is easy to talk about love, but when you stop and think about the magnitude of God's love for us, it is overwhelming. Romans 8:38-39 assures us that nothing can separate us from the love of God in Christ Jesus: "For I am convinced that neither death nor life, neither angels nor demons, neither the present nor the future, nor any powers, neither height nor depth, nor anything else in all creation, will be able to separate us from the love of God that is in Christ Jesus our Lord." This love is not based on our performance, our ability to be good enough, or our successes. It is unconditional, unchanging, and eternal.

Think about that for a moment. We live in a world that constantly demands us to prove our worth, to perform, to live up to expectations, whether they are placed on us by society, by others, or even by ourselves. But in Christ, we are loved simply because we belong to Him. We do not have to earn His love, and we certainly cannot lose it. This kind of love creates a foundation for our lives that is unshakable. When we truly understand that we are fully accepted by God, we can stop striving for the approval of others. We are free to live authentically, knowing that our worth is already secure.

Forgiven and Free

Another beautiful aspect of our new identity in Christ is the freedom we experience. Through Jesus, we are forgiven, not just of the sins we have committed in the past, but also those we struggle with today and will face in the future. Ephesians 1:7-8 reminds us, "In Him we have redemption through His blood, the forgiveness of sins, in accordance with the riches of God's grace that He lavished on us." This forgiveness is total and complete. It is not dependent on our ability to clean ourselves up or make things right. It is purely a result of Jesus' sacrifice on the cross.

But this forgiveness is more than just a theological concept; it is deeply practical. How often do we carry around the weight of guilt and shame from our past? How many times do we replay our failures in our minds, wondering if we will ever be free from the mistakes we have made? The good news is that in Christ, we *are* free. Romans 8:1 tells us, "Therefore, there is now no condemnation for those who are in Christ Jesus." We are no longer defined by the things we have done wrong. We are no longer enslaved to the power of sin, guilt, or shame. We are forgiven and free to live in the fullness of God's grace.

This freedom also means we can be real about our struggles. We do not have to hide behind a mask of perfection, pretending we have it all together. Instead, we can be honest about our brokenness, knowing that our identity is not in our failures but in the forgiveness and freedom Christ has given us.

Empowered and Equipped by the Holy Spirit

God does not just give us a new identity and then leave us to figure it out on our own. He gives us His Holy Spirit to empower and equip us for the life He has called us to live. John 14:26 says,

"But the Advocate, the Holy Spirit, whom the Father will send in My name, will teach you all things and will remind you of everything I have said to you." The Holy Spirit is our constant companion, guiding us, teaching us, and giving us the strength we need to walk in our new identity.

What is incredible about this is that we are not just saved *from* something (our sin, guilt, and brokenness), but we are also saved *for* something. Ephesians 2:10 says, "For we are God's handiwork, created in Christ Jesus to do good works, which God prepared in advance for us to do." God has a plan and a purpose for each of us, and He equips us with everything we need to fulfill that purpose. Whether it is through the gifts He has given us, the opportunities He places before us, or the people He brings into our lives, God is actively working in us and through us to accomplish His will.

Nevertheless, it is important to remember that this empowerment comes from Him, not from us. It is easy to fall into the trap of thinking we need to muster up the strength to live the Christian life on our own. Although the truth is, we cannot do it in our own power. We need the Holy Spirit to guide us, to give us wisdom, and to strengthen us when we feel weak. Acts 1:8 says, "But you will receive power when the Holy Spirit comes on you; and you will be my witnesses in Jerusalem, and in all Judea and Samaria, and to the ends of the earth." This power is not just for a select few. It is for all who belong to Christ.

The Good News Gives Us a Mission

The good news of Jesus Christ does not just change who we are. It completely redefines the purpose of our lives. It invites us into a mission that is far greater than anything we could dream up for ourselves. When we come to know the transforming power of Christ, we are not meant to keep that to ourselves. We are called to be ambassadors of His grace, carriers of the message of reconciliation, and living testimonies of what God has done in our lives. This is not just a suggestion—it is a calling. We are sent into the world to reflect the love of Christ in both word and action.

Living for God's Glory

At the core of our mission is a simple but profound truth: we are called to live for God's glory. 1 Corinthians 10:31 reminds us, "So whether you eat or drink or whatever you do, do it all for the glory of God." Everything we do, whether big or small, has the potential to bring honor and praise to God. The way we work, how we treat others, how we handle challenges, all of it is an opportunity to reflect God's character and point others toward Him.

Living for God's glory is not about performing or striving to earn His approval. It is about recognizing that our lives belong to Him, and that every aspect of our existence: our work, relationships, talents, and daily choices can be used to reflect His goodness and grace. Colossians 3:17 encourages us, "And whatever you do, whether in word or deed, do it all in the name of the Lord Jesus, giving thanks to God the Father through Him."

Living for God's glory means being intentional about the way we live and choosing to honor Him in how we make decisions, how we interact with others, and how we approach life's challenges. Living for God's glory does not have to be church or ministry activities. Living for God's glory is seeing every moment of your life as an opportunity to reflect Christ.

When we live for God's glory, people around us take notice. Our lives become a testimony to the reality of Christ, and others are drawn to the hope, peace, and purpose that we have in Him. This is the kind of life that points others to Jesus, not through flashy words or grand gestures, but through a consistent, humble pursuit of honoring Him in all that we do.

Embracing the Good News

The good news of Jesus Christ is the greatest story ever told. It is the story of a God who loves us so much that He came down to die for us. It is the story of redemption, hope, and new life. The grace of God is what sets Christianity apart from all other world-views and religions. We are not called to earn His favor but simply to receive the gift He offers us through His Son.

Like the transformation we see in Jean Valjean in *Les Misérables*, the Gospel has the power to radically change our lives. Valjean's life was completely altered when he encountered grace, and so too are our lives changed when we encounter the grace of God in Jesus Christ. This grace liberates us, restores us, and empowers us to live lives of love, purpose, and freedom.

As we move forward in our journey of faith, let the Gospel be the foundation upon which we build our lives. Let it be the guiding light that shapes our actions, decisions, and relationships. In Christ, we find everything we need: grace, forgiveness, purpose, and hope.

May we live in the light of His love, sharing this good news with a world that desperately needs to hear it.

SUMMARY OF KEY POINTS

• The Gospel is a proclamation of what Christ has done for us, not what we must do.

• Salvation is a gift of grace, given through the finished work of Jesus on the cross.

• Through Jesus' life, death, and resurrection, we are reconciled to God, forgiven of our sins, and given eternal life.

• The great exchange: Jesus took our sin, and we received His righteousness.

- Living in the light of the good news transforms our lives and frees us from striving for God's approval.

- Our new identity in Christ means we are loved, accepted, forgiven, and equipped by God's Spirit.

- The Gospel gives us a mission: to share the message of Jesus, love our neighbors, and live for God's glory.

REFLECTION QUESTIONS

1. How does understanding the Gospel as "good news" change your perspective on faith and religion?

2. In what areas of your life do you still feel pressure to earn God's approval? How can the message of the Gospel free you from this burden?

3. How does knowing you are fully loved and accepted by God impact your relationships with others?

ACTION STEPS

- Take time this week to read key Gospel passages such as John 3:16-17, Ephesians 2:8-9, and Romans 8:1-2. Reflect on what these verses mean for your life and how they illustrate the good news of Jesus Christ.

- Write down three things you are grateful for that relate to your new identity in Christ. This could be forgiveness, peace, love, or anything else that stands out to you.

- Think of someone in your life who might benefit from hearing the good news. Share your personal story of how the Gospel has changed your life. Remember, it is not about having all the answers but about sharing your genuine experience with others.

PART 3

Application

CHAPTER 7

Understanding Suffering and God's Control

Suffering is a reality we all wish we could avoid, but we cannot. Whether it is personal loss, health struggles, or simply the hardships that life throws our way, suffering is a part of the human experience. If you are like me, you have wondered why. Why do we have to go through pain? Why does God allow it? These questions have been around for as long as people have faced difficulty.

I have had my fair share of suffering, from panic attacks that left me feeling like I was suffocating to a cancer scare that made me face my own mortality. There were moments I asked God, "Why me? What did I do wrong?" Except through these experiences, I have come to understand something that is both hard and freeing: suffering is not always due to something we did. It is often part of a bigger story we cannot fully see yet.

Although here is where it gets tough. We want answers. We want to know why God allows certain things to happen, especially when we are doing everything right. The Bible does not shy away from these questions. In fact, it gives us one of the most powerful stories of suffering in the book of Job.

The Story of Job: A Lesson in Faith During Tough Times

Let's dive into Job's story for a moment because his journey gives us one of the most raw, honest portrayals of human suffering. Job was a good man, a righteous man who loved God and lived a life of integrity. Yet, despite all of this, Job's world fell apart. He lost everything. His wealth, his children, his health were all gone in an instant. If anyone had a reason to question God, it was Job.

Job's suffering was not a result of anything he had done wrong. In fact, it all started with a challenge between Satan and God. Satan basically said, Job only loves You because his life is easy. Take it all away, and he will curse You to Your face. God allowed Satan to test Job, but with limits. Job could lose everything, but his life was spared.

Job then certainly lost everything. Imagine waking up one day and hearing that your entire livelihood is gone, that your children have died in a tragic accident, and then, to top it off, your body is covered in painful sores. That was Job's reality. His pain was so intense that he wished he had never been born. He cried out to God asking why? He did not understand why such terrible things were happening to him when he had lived a life faithful to God.

To make matters worse, Job's friends showed up not to comfort him, but to accuse him. You must have sinned, they said. This kind of suffering only happens to people who deserve it. Although Job knew that was not true. He had not done anything to warrant this kind of devastation, and yet there he was, sitting in the ashes of his former life.

Job's Lament: Pouring Out His Heart to God

One of the things I love most about Job is his honesty with God. Job did not sugarcoat his pain. He laid it all out: his anger, his confusion, his deep sense of abandonment. He cried out, asking why God had allowed this to happen. And in his lament, we find something so profoundly human, the desire to understand the purpose of our suffering.

We have all been there. In those dark moments, we want answers. We want to know why. We want to know the purpose behind the pain. Job discovered the hard truth that sometimes we do not get the answers we are seeking.

When God finally responded to Job, He did not give a detailed explanation of why Job had suffered. Instead, He reminded Job of His power, His wisdom, and the vastness of the universe that Job could not possibly comprehend. God asked Job, "Where were you when I laid the earth's foundation? . . . Who shut up the sea behind doors when it burst forth from the womb?" (Job 38:4, 8, NIV). In other words, Job, there is so much more going on here than you can see.

Here are a few different perspectives to interpret suffering.

The Refiner's Fire: God's Purpose in Suffering

This brings me to the Refiner's Fire analogy. When we are in the midst of suffering, it can feel like we are being burned, like life is heating up to unbearable levels. The pain is intense, and we want out. However, the refining process is not meant to destroy us; it is meant to purify us.

When gold is refined, it is placed in intense heat. The heat caused the impurities to rise to the surface where they are skimmed off, leaving behind pure, valuable gold. The gold does not go through the fire to be ruined; it goes through the fire to become more beautiful, more valuable.

In our lives, suffering can feel like that fire. The heat of trials brings out the impurities: our fears, our doubts, our pride. As painful as it is, God is at work in the process, skimming off those impurities and refining us into something more beautiful than we were before. It is not that God *causes* all our suffering, but He *uses* it to shape us, to make us more like Him.

The Bible tells us that God "sits as a refiner and purifier of silver" (Malachi 3:3, NIV). He is not absent during our suffering. He is right there, carefully watching over the process, ensuring that the heat is not more than we can bear, and working to bring something beautiful out of it.

The Sculptor at Work: God's Chisel

Another metaphor that helps me make sense of suffering is the Sculptor and the Marble. Picture a block of marble in the hands of a skilled sculptor. At first glance, it is just a rough, unshaped block. But the sculptor sees something within it, an image, a masterpiece. He begins to chip away at the marble, piece by piece, until the shape starts to emerge. It is not a gentle process. Each strike of the chisel sends pieces of marble flying, and from the outside, it might seem destructive. But with each strike, the sculptor is getting closer to revealing the masterpiece within.

In the same way, God is our sculptor. He sees the potential in us, the person He created us to be. But sometimes, there are things in our lives that need to be chipped away, things like pride, selfishness, and fear. The process is painful. Each trial feels like a strike of the chisel, and we may not always understand why it is happening. God is not chipping away at us to harm us. He is sculpting us into something beautiful, something that reflects His image more clearly.

The Contrast: Loki's Timekeepers vs. a Loving Sculptor

In the Loki series, the Timekeepers controlled time and destiny with cold, manipulative precision. They were detached; puppeteering lives for their own purposes. And when Loki discovered that his grand ambitions were being controlled by these emotionless forces, he felt robbed of purpose. He struggled with the idea that his life was not his own to control.

Here is where God is so different from the Timekeepers. God's control over our lives is not about manipulation. He is not a detached puppet master pulling the strings from afar. Instead, He is a loving Father, a skilled Sculptor, intimately involved in every detail of our lives. He is not forcing us into a pre-determined role for His own amusement. He is lovingly shaping us into the people we are meant to be, and He is doing it with our good in mind.

God's control is about love. It is about purpose. It is about creating something beautiful out of the broken pieces of our lives. While Loki was left feeling powerless and frustrated under the cold control of the Timekeepers, we can trust in God's plans for us.

Trusting the Process

What does this mean for us in our day-to-day lives? It means that when we go through suffering, we do not have to understand all the reasons why. It is okay to question. It is okay to cry out to God like Job did. But in the end, we are invited to trust that God is at work, refining us, sculpting us, and using even our deepest pain to bring about something good.

I do not have all the answers to why each of our individual sufferings happen, but we know the ultimate cause is sin entering the world. We know during suffering that God loves us and is with us. He is neither distant nor indifferent. He chose to enter the fire and suffer with us to redeem us.

SUMMARY OF KEY POINTS

- Job's suffering reminds us that sometimes we will not get the answers we seek, but we are called to trust God's wisdom and goodness.

- God allows suffering to refine us, burning away impurities and leaving something purer and more valuable behind.

- God, like a sculptor, uses suffering to chip away at what does not belong, revealing the masterpiece He is creating within us.

- Unlike the cold, detached control of Loki's Timekeepers, God's control is rooted in love, purpose, and our ultimate good.

- While we may not understand the reasons behind our suffering, we can trust that God is at work, refining and shaping us for a greater purpose.

REFLECTION QUESTIONS

1. How does Job's story change the way you view your own suffering?

2. In what areas of your life do you feel like you are in the Refiner's Fire or under the Sculptor's chisel?

3. How can you shift your mindset to see God's control as loving and purposeful, rather than distant or manipulative?

4. What impurities do you think God is refining in you through your current struggles?

ACTION STEPS

- Write about a recent experience of suffering and consider how God might be using it to refine or shape you.

- Take time to pray, asking God for the trust to endure the refining process and the chiseling, knowing He is shaping you for good.

- When you face trials, seek God's presence through scripture, worship, and prayer, trusting that He is with you even in the hardest moments.

CHAPTER 8

Humble Confidence

As we continue this journey together, I want to share something foundational to understanding faith: we all have faith in something, religious or not. Faith is a deep trust or confidence in something or someone, often beyond what can be fully seen or proven.

> "You can't get through life without faith. Even the most secular, materialistic people build their lives on a faith commitment to certain assumptions about life and the universe that can't be proved." —Tim Keller

My belief in the Gospel of Jesus Christ—that He died for our sins, rose from the dead, and is Lord of all—stems from a combination of study, experiences, historical evidence, and, ultimately, faith. But I have also come to realize that faith is not a concept unique to Christianity; it is something every person engages with, often unconsciously. Many people go through life living with unexamined convictions, trusting in a worldview that has been shaped for them by the prevailing culture, family upbringing, or personal aspirations.

For anyone who does not consider themselves a person of faith, the reality is that we all are already making decisions rooted in faith, whether we realize it or not. So the real question becomes: *Where are you placing your trust?* Is it in your career, relationships, personal abilities, scientific progress, or in something greater than yourself? These beliefs, whether consciously chosen or passively inherited, shape your worldview, the way you live, and the meaning you derive from life.

For Christians, our confidence is rooted in the truth revealed through Jesus Christ. Yet this confidence is not about having all the answers or proving others wrong. We can trust that God's plan is infinitely greater than what we can fully understand. We are freed to extend grace, love, and empathy to others when we share our faith, remembering that our faith is centered on dependence on Christ and not self-reliance.

In Proverbs 3:5-6, we are encouraged to "Trust in the Lord with all your heart and lean not on your own understanding; in all your ways submit to Him, and He will make your paths straight." This kind of trust requires humility. It means acknowledging that we do not have all the answers, but we believe that God does. Surrendering our desire to control every outcome and instead, walking in the confidence that God's wisdom is guiding us, even when we do not see the full picture.

As we explore this chapter, I invite you to reflect on where you have placed your trust. Consider whether the foundation you have built your life upon is utterly secure. My hope is that you will find, as I have, that humble confidence is found not in our own strength or understanding but in trusting a God who knows the way forward, even when we do not.

Lean Not on Your Own Understanding

The Parable of the Blind Men and the Elephant

One of the greatest challenges in life is realizing how limited our perspectives can be. This is illustrated in an ancient parable about several blind men encountering an elephant for the first time. Each man touches a different part of the elephant. One feels the leg and believes the elephant is a tree, another feels the trunk and thinks it is a snake, and another feels the tusk and concludes it is a spear. Each one is convinced that his perspective is the whole truth, but they are each only grasping a piece of the full picture. You may have heard this parable used to say all religions are the same, all partial answers. But that misses the centerpiece of the parable, the elephant! There is a real truth that is beyond the limits of any of the humans to understand.

This parable reminds us of the limits of our own understanding. In our finite human experience, it is easy to assume that our perspective is the complete truth. But as Christians, we know that while our understanding is limited, God has revealed the bigger picture (the elephant) through Jesus Christ. Jesus said, "I am the way and the truth and the life. No one comes to the Father except through me" (John 14:6, NIV). We cannot reach the whole truth ourselves, but God has brought it to us.

Our confidence in Christ does not come from knowing everything. It comes from trusting that God's truth is enough to give clarity to life's biggest questions. Even as we hold onto that confidence, we must do so with humility, recognizing that we are all still learning and growing. As 1 Corinthians 13:12 reminds us, "For now we see only a reflection as in a mirror; then we shall see face to face. Now I know in part; then I shall know fully, even as I am fully known."

Plato's Allegory of the Cave

Plato's *Allegory of the Cave* offers another vivid illustration of how limited our perspectives can be. In the allegory, prisoners are chained inside a dark cave, able only to see shadows projected on the wall by objects behind them. To these prisoners, the shadows are reality. They believe they are seeing the entirety of the world. However, when one prisoner is freed and steps outside, he discovers a world far greater and more vibrant than the shadows he had once thought were everything.

Faith in Jesus is like stepping out of that cave. It recognizes that there is more to life than the shadows we have known. Faith enables us to see beyond the temporary, beyond the limitations of our understanding, and into the fullness of what God has prepared for us. "For now, we see only a reflection as in a mirror; then we shall see face to face" (1 Corinthians 13:12, NIV). We may not have all the answers now, but we have the assurance that God's truth is leading us toward a deeper reality. One that transcends what we can see or comprehend.

Confidence Rooted in God's Truth

For Christians, confidence does not come from understanding every mystery of the universe. Confidence comes from trusting in the truth revealed through Jesus Christ. Ephesians 2:10 tells us, "For we are God's handiwork, created in Christ Jesus to do good works, which God prepared in advance for us to do." This means that our purpose is already part of God's plan. We do not need to have everything figured out. God has already set a path for us.

This is where true confidence lies—not in knowing all the steps ahead but in trusting that God has prepared the way. However, this confidence should always be accompanied by humility. Confidence in God does not mean arrogance or superiority. Instead, it means that God's plan is greater than what we can understand and knowing that we are called to serve others with love and grace. James 4:6 reminds us, "God opposes the proud but shows favor to the humble."

Faith Grows in Unseen Ways

Faith often grows quietly, beneath the surface, much like the Chinese bamboo tree. After planting the seed for the bamboo tree, there is no visible growth above the ground for several years. But during that time, the bamboo is developing a deep and extensive root system underground. Then, seemingly overnight, the tree shoots up and grows rapidly.

In the same way, our faith can sometimes feel stagnant, as though nothing is happening. Although God is at work within us, developing our character, deepening our trust in Him, and preparing us for growth that we may not yet see. Philippians 1:6 encourages us with this truth: "He who began a good work in you will carry it on to completion until the day of Christ Jesus."

In my own life, there have been seasons where I could not see any visible progress. I felt like I was doing all the right things: praying, trusting, seeking God's will, but nothing seemed to change. It was only in hindsight that I could see how God was growing my faith in unseen ways preparing me for future seasons of fruitfulness. If you are in a season where growth feels slow or invisible, trust that God is still working. Faith often grows in ways we cannot see, and God's work in you will be revealed in His perfect timing.

Christ-Reliance over Self-Reliance

In Disney's *Moana*, we follow the story of a young girl wrestling with her own doubts and questions about her calling. She feels the weight of her family's and community's expectations and wonders whether she is really the one destined to restore the heart of Te Fiti. Throughout her journey, Moana is driven by a need to discover who she is and to prove to herself and others that she is enough. As she embraces her path, she gains confidence, not because she knows exactly where it will lead, but because she starts to trust in herself and the legacy of her ancestors.

Her story resonates with many of us. We, too, have moments where we feel drawn to something greater but question whether we have what it takes. We wonder if we are truly equipped for the challenges before us, just like Moana, who questions her ability to carry out her mission. These doubts can feel paralyzing at times and leave us asking, *Am I really the right person for this?*

However as much as Moana's journey mirrors our struggles, there is a fundamental difference between her story and the journey of faith we are called to as followers of Christ. Moana finds strength by looking within, discovering that she has always been enough. The Christian life, however, calls us to a different truth. Our strength comes not from self-discovery or self-reliance but from a deep dependence on Christ.

While Moana's journey is centered on human capability and self-actualization, the path of a believer rests in knowing that our confidence does not come from what we can muster on our own. It comes from Christ who is the author of our story. We are not the heroes; He is. Our calling and purpose are not something we have to prove but something we step into because of what He has already accomplished for us. In Moana's case, the resolution is found in her realization that she has always been enough. For us, the journey starts with the recognition that we are not enough on our own. That is why we need Jesus.

Unlike Moana, who searches for her identity within herself, we are called to trust that God has already laid out the path for us. Our confidence does not come from knowing all the details, it comes from trusting in the One who has already walked the road ahead of us and who equips us for what He has called us to do.

Moana's journey reflects a common theme we see in the world around us, the belief that we must find our own meaning, identity, and strength. It is an inspiring message in some ways, but it falls short of the truth we find in the Gospel. Our culture often tells us to rely on ourselves, but Jesus calls us to rely on Him. He reminds us in John 15:5, "I am the vine; you are the branches. If you remain in me and I in you, you will bear much fruit; apart from me, you can do nothing." The stark contrast is clear. Moana succeeds through self-reliance. We find our true fulfillment only through dependence on Christ.

It is easy to get caught up in the idea that we must be self-sufficient or capable of doing anything if we just try hard enough. But the Gospel flips that narrative on its head. It invites us to acknowledge our weakness and to trust fully in God's strength. As Paul says in 2 Corinthians 12:9, "My grace is sufficient for you, for my power is made perfect in weakness." Our weakness does not disqualify us. It becomes the very place where God's power is most fully displayed.

Unlike Moana, whose journey leads her to embrace her own capabilities, we are invited to embrace something much greater, a life of surrender to Christ. When we face doubt or fear, we do not need to look inward for strength. Instead, we look to Jesus, the One who has already secured our identity, our purpose, and our future. The world may tell us to strive for self-reliance, but the Gospel calls us to rest in the One who is all-sufficient.

In the end, Moana's story can inspire us to step into the unknown, but as followers of Christ, our journey requires more than self-trust. It calls for a heart fully surrendered to God, knowing that He goes before us, walks beside us, and strengthens us for every step of the journey. Our confidence does not come from what we can accomplish; it comes from the One who has already accomplished everything on our behalf. That is the difference between a journey of self-reliance and a journey dependent on Christ.

Living with Humble Confidence

Living with humble confidence is acknowledging that we all make faith-based decisions, whether we realize it or not. We do not need to have all the answers but can trust in God's truth while extending grace and empathy to others.

We are not called to prove ourselves or force others to adopt our views. Instead, we are called to live out our faith with love and authenticity, reflecting God's grace in the way we engage with those around us. Confidence in Christ should always walk hand in hand with humility, making space for meaningful conversations and genuine care for others. As 1 Peter 3:15 says, "Always be prepared to give an answer to everyone who asks you to give the reason for the hope that you have. But do this with gentleness and respect."

SUMMARY OF KEY POINTS

- Everyone makes faith-based decisions, whether religious or not. We all place our trust in something beyond ourselves.

- Christian confidence is rooted in God's truth revealed through Christ, but it must always be balanced with humility, love, and empathy for others.

- God is working beneath the surface, often in unseen ways, developing our faith over time like the growth of the bamboo tree.

REFLECTION QUESTIONS

1. Where in your life do you feel God is calling you to step out in faith, even if you do not have all the answers?

2. How does knowing that everyone makes faith-based decisions change the way you view others who may believe differently?

3. What would your life look like if you trusted God with your doubts and uncertainties? How would it change the way you approach challenges?

ACTION STEP

- This week, reflect on an area of your life where you have been holding back because of doubt or fear. Write down one action you can take in faith, trusting that God has equipped you for the journey ahead. Share this step with someone in your community for encouragement and accountability.

CHAPTER 9

The End of Self-Righteousness

If the good news is truly about what Christ has done for us, and not about what we have done to earn anything, then we must start with the end of self-righteousness. The Gospel is not meant to create Christians who walk around thinking they have achieved some special standing with God through their own efforts. Instead, it is meant to bring us to a place of total reliance on Christ's righteousness, which fosters humility, dependence on God's grace, and freedom to love others without needing anything in return. It is not about us; it is all about Him.

A Lesson in Self Righteousness

We see this clearly in the parable of the prodigal son (Luke 15:11-32). The focus is often on the younger son, who essentially tells his father, "I wish you were dead" by asking for his inheritance early. He takes the money and squanders it on wild, reckless living. Then, in his brokenness, he realizes his mistake and decides to return home, fully expecting to beg his father to let him be a servant. But his father, defying all cultural norms, runs out to meet him, throws his arms around him, and throws a party to celebrate his return. This is grace: unearned, undeserved, but lavishly given.

However, we cannot overlook the older brother's part in this story. He represents the self-righteousness we are talking about here. He stayed behind, did all the right things, obeyed his father, and was angry when his younger brother, who wasted everything, was welcomed back with open arms. The older brother felt like he deserved better because of his own efforts. But his father gently reminds him that he has always had everything. He just did not see it. He was relying on his own good behavior instead of recognizing his father's grace that had been available to him all along.

This parable beautifully illustrates that being "good enough" does not earn us anything from God. Rather accepting God's grace, whether you have been reckless or have tried to be obedient your whole life, makes you his son or daughter. Both sons needed their father's love, and both needed to understand that their standing was not based on their actions but on their father's grace.

Redeemed, Not "Good" People Go to Heaven

Let's take this a step further. It is not good people who go to heaven, but redeemed people who accept Christ. The truth is, even those who try their hardest to live a good life fall short of God's standard. Romans 3:23 makes it clear: "For all have sinned and fall short of the glory of God." The reality is, no matter how "good" we think we are, we all miss the mark. Here is where it gets challenging for many people: As scandalous as it may seem, someone on death row who accepts Christ's perfection is better off than someone who tries to live a moral life apart from Him. None of us can meet God's perfect standard without Jesus.

This reality is echoed in the story of the Pharisees, the religious leaders of Jesus' day. They knew God's law and tried to obey it, but they used it as a measure of their own righteousness rather than relying on God's grace. Jesus was blunt with them: "Woe to you, teachers of the law and Pharisees, you hypocrites! You are like whitewashed tombs, which look beautiful on the outside but on the inside are full of the bones of the dead and everything unclean" (Matthew 23:27-28). This is what self-righteousness looks like, clean on the outside, dead on the inside. True righteousness does not come from following the rules but from being transformed by grace, which is illustrated in the stories below.

The Pharisee and the Tax Collector

Jesus made this point even more explicitly in the parable of the Pharisee and the tax collector (Luke 18:9-14). The Pharisee stood in the temple and thanked God that he was not like other people: robbers, evildoers, or even the tax collector standing nearby. He listed his religious achievements, fasting twice a week and giving a tenth of everything he earned, but the tax collector stood at a distance. He would not even look up to heaven. He simply prayed, "God, have mercy on me, a sinner."

Jesus' conclusion was shocking to His listeners. It was the tax collector, not the Pharisee, who went home justified before God. The Pharisee, with all his outward righteousness, missed the point entirely. He was relying on his own goodness, while the tax collector knew he had nothing to offer but a plea for mercy. This parable drives home the futility of self-righteousness and the power of humble reliance on God's grace.

The Thief on the Cross

One of the most powerful demonstrations of grace is found in the story of the thief on the cross (Luke 23:39-43). As Jesus was being crucified, two criminals were executed alongside Him. One mocked Jesus, demanding that He save Himself and them if He was truly the Messiah. But the other thief rebuked him, saying, "Don't you fear God? We are punished justly, for we are getting what our deeds deserve. But this man has done nothing wrong." Then he turned to Jesus and said, "Remember me when you come into your kingdom."

Jesus' response is breathtaking: "Truly I tell you, today you will be with me in paradise." Here was a man with no opportunity to clean up his act, no time to earn his way into heaven. His salvation was purely an act of grace, a gift freely given in response to his faith. It is a stark reminder that salvation is not something we earn. It is something we receive.

Paul: A Life Transformed by Grace

The Apostle Paul's life is another powerful testimony to the transformative power of grace. Before his encounter with Christ, Paul (then Saul) a zealous Pharisee convinced that he was doing God's will, persecuted Christians. But after his dramatic conversion on the road to Damascus (Acts 9), Paul's life radically changed. He went from being a legalistic persecutor of the church to one of its most passionate advocates of grace.

Paul never forgot where he came from. He often referred to himself as the "chief of sinners" (1 Timothy 1:15). Except rather than being weighed down by guilt, Paul was liberated by grace. He understood better than most that his righteousness did not come from his own efforts but from Christ's sacrifice. As he wrote in Philippians 3:8-9, "I consider everything a loss because of the surpassing worth of knowing Christ Jesus my Lord . . . not having a righteousness of my own that comes from the law, but that which is through faith in Christ."

The Temptation of Legalism

Even though we know that salvation comes by grace through faith, legalism can still creep into our thinking. Legalism is the mindset that our relationship with God depends on how well we follow the rules. It shifts our focus away from Christ's finished work and puts it back on our own efforts. We begin to believe that if we just try harder, pray more, or sin less, then God will be pleased with us.

Nevertheless, the Gospel leaves no room for legalism. Paul addressed this issue head-on in his letter to the Galatians, where some believers were being told that faith in Christ was not enough; they also needed to follow the Jewish law. Paul's response was blunt: "It is for freedom that Christ has set us free. Stand firm, then, and do not let yourselves be burdened again by a yoke of slavery" (Galatians 5:1). In other words, do not go back to trying to earn what Christ has already freely given you.

Legalism does not just distort our relationship with God; it also distorts how we view others. When we rely on our own righteousness, we tend to look down on those who do not measure up. But grace humbles us, reminding us that we are all in need of mercy. It frees us to love others without judgment, knowing that we are no better than anyone else. We are just recipients of God's unearned favor.

Jesus' Confrontation of Legalism

Throughout His ministry, Jesus regularly confronted the legalism of the Pharisees. These religious leaders prided themselves on their strict observance of the law, but Jesus saw through their outward displays of righteousness. In Matthew 23:27, He called them "whitewashed tombs," beautiful on the outside, but full of death on the inside. They followed the letter of the law but missed the heart of it.

Jesus did not confront the Pharisees because they were trying to obey God. He confronted them because they were using their obedience to prop up their own self-righteousness. They had missed the point of the law, which was always meant to point people to their need for a Savior. Jesus' harshest words were reserved for those who thought they did not need grace.

Christianity: Grace over Works

This is where Christianity stands out in stark contrast to most other world religions. Many religions operate on a system of works. If you do enough good, you will be rewarded. Whether it is karma in Hinduism, where your actions determine your future reincarnations, or Islam, where your virtuous deeds must outweigh your bad ones, the focus is on earning favor. But Christianity is different. It says, "It is finished" (John 19:30). The work has already been done. Salvation is a gift.

The Freedom of Grace

Grace sets us free. Romans 6:14 tells us, "For sin shall no longer be your master, because you are not under the law, but under grace." Grace frees us from the endless cycle of trying to be good enough. It liberates us from the anxiety of wondering if we have done enough to earn God's favor. It allows us to rest in the finished work of Christ.

However, grace does not mean we can live however we want. It transforms us from the inside out. Titus 2:11-12 says, "For the grace of God has appeared that offers salvation to all people. It teaches us to say 'No' to ungodliness and worldly passions, and to live self-controlled, upright, and godly lives in this present age." Grace empowers us to live for God, not because we are trying to earn anything but because we have been set free to live the life we were created for.

Walking in Humility

Grace should lead us to humility. It is easy, once we have experienced God's grace, to become prideful about it, to look down on those who have not yet grasped the freedom of the Gospel. But grace does not lead to arrogance; it leads to deep humility. We did not earn this gift, and we have no reason to boast.

Philippians 2:3-4 reminds us, "Do nothing out of selfish ambition or vain conceit. Rather, in humility value others above yourselves." Grace frees us from the need to prove ourselves, and that allows us to love others more fully. It allows us to extend the same grace we have received to those around us, even those who are still struggling to find their way.

Living in the Light of Grace

When we embrace the truth that it is not good people who go to heaven but redeemed people who accept Christ, it changes everything. We are set free from the exhausting pursuit of trying to earn God's favor. We can rest in the assurance that our salvation is secure because of what Jesus has done.

This assurance does not lead to complacency; it leads to worship, gratitude, and a life of service to God and others. The Gospel transforms how we see ourselves and how we see others. It removes the need for comparison or judgment and replaces it with a desire to see others experience the same grace we have found.

As we live in the light of this grace, we become beacons of hope, pointing others to the redeeming love of Jesus. Our righteousness is found in Christ alone, and because of that, we have a hope and a future that is secure.

SUMMARY OF KEY POINTS

- The parable of the prodigal son and other biblical stories show that it is not about being good enough—it is about being redeemed.

- True righteousness comes from Christ, not our own efforts. We are seen as righteous in God's eyes because of what Jesus has done, not because of anything we can do.

- Embracing this truth fosters humility and reliance on God's grace, transforming our relationships and encouraging us to extend grace and love to others as we have received it.

- Legalism and self-righteousness are contrary to the Gospel message. Our hope and assurance come from Christ's finished work, not from our ability to follow rules or earn God's favor.

- The Gospel calls us to respond with worship, gratitude, and a life devoted to loving God and others.

REFLECTION QUESTIONS

1. Where do you see self-righteousness at work in your own life? How might you be tempted to rely on your own efforts, rather than Christ's finished work?

2. How does understanding Christ's righteousness change the way you approach your faith and daily life?

3. In what ways can you extend grace to others, knowing that you have received grace freely from God?

4. How does the concept that "redeemed people, not good people, go to heaven" challenge or comfort you?

ACTION STEPS

- This week, choose one area of your life where you often feel the need to prove yourself or earn approval. Consciously rely on God's grace in that area, reminding yourself that your worth and acceptance come from Christ, not your performance.

- Take time this week to reflect on God's grace in your life. Write down specific ways God has shown you grace and how it has transformed you.

CHAPTER 10

Living in freedom

C hrist came to set us free. This freedom is not merely a release
from physical or external constraints; it is a deep, spiritual liberation from the burdens that weigh down our souls: our striving
for approval, our endless pursuit of validation, and our desperate
attempts to measure up in a broken world. True freedom in Christ
is more than the absence of chains. It is the invitation to live fully
as we were created to live loved, secure, and at peace with God.

The Matrix: An Analogy of Freedom

A powerful modern analogy for this kind of liberation can be
found in the movie *The Matrix*. In the film, Neo is trapped in
a world that appears real but is, in fact, an artificial construct
designed to keep humanity enslaved. The world of *The Matrix*
mirrors the illusion many people live in today. A reality defined
by striving for success, validation, and meaning through external

means. Much like the characters in *The Matrix*, we are often oblivious to the true reality of our spiritual condition.

When Neo takes the red pill, he is awakened to the truth. The layers of deception are peeled away, and he begins to see the world as it really is full of brokenness and control. This awakening reflects the moment when someone encounters Christ and their eyes are opened to the truth of the Gospel. Jesus is, in many ways, the "red pill" that reveals the reality of sin, death, and the need for salvation.

Before Neo's awakening he is like many of us, unaware of his captivity. He goes through life thinking he is free but is bound by unseen forces. Similarly, many people live under the illusion of freedom while being enslaved by sin, fear, and the relentless pursuit of worldly approval. True freedom begins when we recognize that we are living in a world of false promises and come to understand that Christ alone can set us free.

Just as Neo had to learn to live in the truth and embrace his identity as "The One," Christians are called to live in the truth of Christ's victory and embrace their identity as children of God. We must let go of the false realities that enslave us: the need to earn God's favor, the pressure to conform to the world's standards, and the fear of not measuring up. In Christ, we are set free to live fully, without fear or shame, knowing that our identity and worth are secure in Him.

What Does This Freedom Mean?

Living in true freedom means embracing the gift that Christ has already given us. It is realizing that we do not have to earn God's love or prove our worth. The world tells us we need to perform, to succeed, to always do more. But Christ tells us, "It is finished." The work is done. He has already secured for us what we could never achieve on our own, a restored relationship with God.

Think about that for a moment. Jesus did not just free us from something. He freed us *for* something. He freed us to live in the fullness of His love, to experience the joy of being called a child of God, and to walk in a peace that surpasses understanding. He freed us to live lives of purpose without the crippling fear of failure or rejection.

Freedom from Sin

One of the greatest aspects of this freedom is our liberation from sin. Jesus declared, "So if the Son sets you free, you will be free indeed" (John 8:36). Sin is no longer our master. Before Christ, we were bound by sin, unable to escape its grip on our lives. We could not break free no matter how hard we tried. But through His death and resurrection, Christ broke the power of sin once and for all. He paid the price that we could never pay, and in doing so, He set us free from the chains of guilt, shame, and condemnation.

This is not just a theological concept; it is a reality we can live in each day. It means that no matter what mistakes we have made, no matter how far we have strayed, we are forgiven. We are free to live without the burden of our past sins hanging over us. We are free to approach God with confidence knowing that we are fully accepted in Christ.

Freedom from Condemnation

There is a powerful freedom that comes from knowing that in Christ we are no longer under condemnation. Romans 8:1 tells us, "Therefore, there is now no condemnation for those who are in Christ Jesus." Think about the weight that lifts from our shoulders when we realize that God is not waiting to condemn us for our failures. Instead, He invites us into His grace.

This does not mean we will not make mistakes or struggle with sin, but it does mean that our failures do not define us. We are defined by the love of Christ by the fact that He took on the punishment we deserved and gave us His righteousness. When God looks at us, He does not see our shortcomings. He sees His beloved children.

This truth changes everything. We no longer must live in fear of judgment or failure. Instead, we are free to live with boldness and confidence, knowing that God's love for us is unwavering, and His grace is always enough.

The Freedom to Love and Serve

Freedom in Christ not only sets us free from sin and condemnation but also enables us to genuinely love and serve others. Galatians 5:13 reminds us, "You, my brothers and sisters, were called to be free. But do not use your freedom to indulge the flesh; rather, serve one another humbly in love."

When we live in the freedom Christ gives us, we are no longer weighed down by selfish desires or a need to prove ourselves. Instead, we are free to turn our attention outward; to love others the way Christ has loved us. This is a freedom that empowers us to make a difference in the lives of those around us, to be a light in a world that desperately needs hope.

This is a beautiful irony: The more we give ourselves away in love and service, the more we experience the true freedom Christ offers. In losing ourselves, we find ourselves. In serving others, we discover the joy and fulfillment that comes from living out our purpose in God's kingdom.

The Role of the Holy Spirit in Our Freedom

This journey of living in true freedom is not one we walk alone. The Holy Spirit is our constant companion, guiding us, strengthening us, and reminding us of the truth of who we are in Christ.

When we accept Jesus, the Holy Spirit dwells in us, and He is the one who empowers us to live out this freedom.

The Spirit gives us the strength to resist the pull of sin and the wisdom to navigate the challenges of life. He produces in us the fruit of the Spirit: love, joy, peace, patience, kindness, goodness, faithfulness, gentleness, and self-control (Galatians 5:22-23). These are the qualities of a life lived in freedom, and they grow in us as we stay connected to the Spirit.

The Holy Spirit is also the one who reminds us of our identity. When the world tries to tell us we are not enough or that we are defined by our past, the Spirit whispers the truth, "You are loved. You are chosen. You are free." He leads us into a deeper understanding of the freedom we have in Christ helping us to live in that freedom every day.

Freedom Is a Journey

While Christ has already won our freedom, living in that freedom is a daily journey. We will face moments when we are tempted to fall back into old patterns of thinking, when we start striving for approval or fall back into guilt and shame. Except the beauty of this journey is that Christ walks with us every step of the way. He invites us to come to Him daily, to rest in His love and remind ourselves of the truth that we are free.

Living in true freedom does not mean life will be without challenges. But it does mean that we face those challenges with a new perspective. We are no longer slaves to fear, worry, or sin. We are children of God, free to live in the fullness of His grace and love.

A Life of Joy and Purpose

This is the life we were meant to live, a life where we are free from the burdens of sin, guilt, and shame. A life where we are free to love and serve others, to live boldly and confidently in the knowledge that we are fully known and fully loved by God. A life where we walk in step with the Holy Spirit, bearing fruit that blesses the world around us.

This is the life of true freedom, and it is available to all who place their trust in Jesus. As we continue this journey, let us hold fast to the truth that Christ has set us free, and in that freedom, let us live lives that reflect His love, grace, and joy.

SUMMARY OF KEY POINTS

- True freedom in Christ is not just freedom from sin, but freedom *for* a life of love, joy, and purpose.

- Freedom from condemnation means we can live without fear of judgment, knowing that we are fully accepted by God.

- The Holy Spirit empowers us to live out this freedom by producing the fruit of the Spirit in our lives.

- Freedom is a journey, and while we may face challenges, we walk in the knowledge that Christ is with us every step of the way.

REFLECTION QUESTIONS

1. In what areas of your life do you still feel bound, despite knowing that Christ has set you free?

2. How does the freedom Christ offers differ from the world's idea of freedom?

3. What doubts or fears hold you back from embracing this freedom?

4. How can you use your freedom in Christ to serve others, rather than for selfish purposes?

ACTION STEPS

- Reflect on the freedom you have in Christ. Spend time in prayer or journaling, thanking God for setting you free from sin and guilt.

- Ask the Holy Spirit to guide you in living out your freedom, especially in loving and serving others.

- Share the message of freedom with someone else who may be struggling to understand or accept it. Offer to pray with them or invite them into a deeper conversation about Christ's love.

PART 4

Implications

CHAPTER 11

Christ is King

The resurrection of Jesus Christ stands as the pivotal event in human history. If we accept that Christ rose from the dead, the implications are both profound and far-reaching. The resurrection is not merely a historical event but the validation of Christ's identity as the Son of God and the confirmation of His authority over all creation. This authority extends to His teachings, which define right and wrong and offer a framework for living a life of purpose, service, and alignment with divine will.

Avengers: Endgame and Christ's Kingship

In *Avengers: Endgame*, the heroes are faced with an impossible situation: half of the universe has been wiped out by Thanos, a powerful antagonist who believes he is bringing balance by destroying lives. The Avengers, each with their own unique abilities and burdens, come together to attempt the impossible, restoring life and undoing the chaos.

Much like how Jesus' kingship is defined by selflessness, humility, and sacrifice, *Endgame* emphasizes the power of sacrificial love. The character of Tony Stark (Iron Man) embodies this principle most powerfully. He is not the strongest Avenger, but he makes the ultimate sacrifice, laying down his life to save the universe. Stark's final act, willingly using the Infinity Stones to reverse Thanos' destruction, knowing it will kill him, mirrors the self-giving love that Christ demonstrated on the cross.

Just as Tony Stark's death restores life to countless beings in the universe, Christ's death and resurrection restored life to humanity. Jesus, like Stark, is a figure who holds immense power but uses that power not for personal gain but for the salvation of others. His kingship is not about domination or control, but about service and self-sacrifice for the good of all.

The Authority of Christ

The resurrection of Christ establishes His supreme authority over all things. This authority means His teachings are not optional guidelines, but divine imperatives meant for our ultimate good. When Jesus commands us to love our enemies, forgive those who wrong us, and seek first the kingdom of God, these are not just moral platitudes. They are the blueprint for living in harmony with God and others. As followers of Christ, we are called to submit to His authority, trusting that His commands lead to life and flourishing, even when they challenge our natural inclinations or societal norms.

Wrestling with Scripture

The Bible, as the inspired Word of God, contains many challenging and perplexing elements. From the Nephilim, giants inhabiting the land (Numbers 13:33), to the mysterious cities Cain fled to after killing Abel (Genesis 4:16-17), and the enigmatic references to the "sons of God" taking human wives (Genesis 6:1-4), Scripture is filled with narratives that stretch our understanding. God destroyed Sodom and Gomorrah by fire because of their wickedness (Genesis 19:24-25) but sent Jonah to rescue the wicked city of Nineveh (Jonah 1:2). Narratives like these seem contradictory and add to the challenge of understanding the Bible.

These passages challenge us intellectually and spiritually. It can be tempting to dismiss them or avoid confronting their implications. However, engaging with these difficult texts is essential for a mature faith. I, too, have wrestled with these stories and teachings. It would be easier to believe that humanity is not inherently sinful or at odds with a holy God. It would be more comfortable to endorse a worldview where everyone is free to live as they please without the constraints of divine judgment. But the reality of sin and the need for redemption are central to the Christian faith, and these truths must be confronted honestly and humbly.

The Purpose and Unity of the Bible

To navigate these challenges, it is crucial to understand the Bible as a unified narrative that tells the story of God's interaction with humanity. The Bible is not a collection of disconnected moral teachings or ancient myths but a coherent story that reveals God's character, His plan for redemption, and His ultimate purpose for creation. From Genesis to Revelation, the Bible speaks of a God who creates, sustains, redeems, and restores. Each part of the Bible must be read considering the whole with an understanding of its historical context and its place in the overarching narrative of salvation.

Moreover, the Bible must be approached with a clear understanding of who God is—He is holy, just, loving, and merciful.

God's self-revelation reaches its climax in the person of Jesus Christ, whose life, death, and resurrection are the ultimate demonstration of God's love and commitment to humanity. Understanding the Bible in this light allows us to see the unity and purpose of Scripture, even in its most challenging passages.

Christ's Elevation of the Marginalized

One of the most revolutionary aspects of Jesus' ministry was His treatment of those whom society had marginalized: women, the poor, and the oppressed. In a culture that often devalued these groups, Jesus consistently elevated their status and affirmed their worth as image-bearers of God.

Women in Jesus' Ministry

In the Gospels, we see Jesus breaking social and religious norms by engaging with women in ways that were considered scandalous by the standards of His day. For example, Jesus had a deep theological conversation with the Samaritan woman at the well (John 4), revealing to her His identity as the Messiah. This was shocking not only because she was a woman but also because she was a Samaritan, a group despised by the Jews. Yet Jesus treated her with dignity and respect, offering her the "living water" of eternal life.

Moreover, women played a crucial role in Jesus' ministry. They were among His closest followers and were the first to witness His resurrection (Mark 16:1-11). In a society where a woman's testimony was often disregarded, the fact that the Gospels emphasize women as the primary witnesses to the resurrection underscores the value Jesus placed on women. He consistently challenged the cultural norms of His time, affirming the dignity, worth, and importance of women in the kingdom of God.

Jesus' Care for the Poor

Jesus also placed a strong emphasis on caring for the poor and marginalized. His teachings often highlighted God's special concern for the needy. In the Beatitudes, Jesus proclaimed, "Blessed are the poor in spirit, for theirs is the kingdom of heaven" (Matthew 5:3), and "Blessed are the meek, for they will inherit the earth" (Matthew 5:5). He urged His followers to care for the "least of these," teaching that when they served the hungry, the thirsty, the stranger, the naked, the sick, and the imprisoned, they were serving Him (Matthew 25:34-40).

Throughout His ministry, Jesus reached out to those on the margins of society, the lepers, the blind, the lame, and the outcasts, offering them healing, hope, and inclusion in the community of God's people. By doing so, He demonstrated that the kingdom of God is open to all, regardless of social status or wealth or political affiliation. His actions laid the foundation for a worldview that values human rights and social justice that is grounded in the belief that every person bears the image of God.

Uplifting the Oppressed

In addition to elevating women and the poor, Jesus championed the cause of the oppressed. He confronted the religious leaders of His day who often exploited their positions of power to oppress the common people. Jesus condemned their hypocrisy calling them "whitewashed tombs" who appeared righteous outwardly but were corrupt within (Matthew 23:27). He advocated for justice, mercy, and faithfulness, and rebuked the legalistic tendencies that burdened people with heavy religious obligations without offering true spiritual liberation.

Moreover, Jesus identified with the oppressed in a profound way. He Himself experienced rejection, suffering, and a brutal execution at the hands of the powerful. Yet, through His death and resurrection, He triumphed over the forces of oppression, sin, and death, offering hope to all who are oppressed. His life and teachings provided the ethical framework that would later inspire movements for social justice and human rights.

Christ as the Fulfillment of the Covenant with Abraham

In the Old Testament, Jesus is foreshadowed as the fulfillment of the covenant God made with Abraham. This covenant, detailed in Genesis 15, was a pivotal moment in the biblical narrative. God promised Abraham that He would make his descendants as numerous as the stars and that through his offspring, all the nations of the earth would be blessed. This promise was sealed with a solemn ceremony where animals were cut in half, and both parties would walk between the pieces, symbolizing the consequences of breaking the covenant; may they be cut in half like the animals if they fail to uphold their part.

However, in a remarkable twist, it is only God, represented by a smoking firepot and a blazing torch, who passes between the pieces. This act signifies that God is taking upon Himself the full responsibility for the fulfillment of the covenant, as well as the consequences of any potential breach. This is an extraordinary demonstration of God's grace and faithfulness.

This covenant ceremony foreshadows Christ's mission. Just as God took upon Himself the covenantal curse, Jesus, in the New Testament, takes upon Himself the curse of sin on behalf of humanity. On the cross, Jesus becomes the sacrificial Lamb, bearing the punishment that we deserve. He embodies the covenant by fulfilling its demands and taking the curse upon Himself, thereby securing the blessings of the covenant for all who trust in Him.

This profound act of love and sacrifice highlights the continuity between the Old and New Testaments and shows that Jesus is the ultimate fulfillment of God's promises to Abraham. Through Christ, the blessings promised to Abraham, righteousness, a multitude of descendants, and a blessing to all nations, are realized. Jesus is the true and better Abraham who mediates a new and everlasting covenant, sealed not with the blood of animals, but with His own precious blood.

Living Selflessly

Christ's kingship calls us to live selflessly. Jesus exemplified this through His life and death. He came not to be served but to serve and to give His life as a ransom for many (Mark 10:45). As His followers, we are called to imitate this example, putting the needs of others before our own. This selfless living is difficult in a world that often values self-interest and personal gain, but it is the path to true fulfillment and purpose. In serving others, we reflect the love and humility of Christ and participate in His redemptive work in the world.

Community and Compassion

Christ's reign emphasizes the importance of community and compassion. Throughout His ministry, Jesus reached out to the marginalized and oppressed, showing love and compassion to those whom society had rejected. If we are to follow His example, we must also reach out to those in need, offering support, kindness, and love. This means not only addressing physical needs but also providing emotional and spiritual support, helping others to see their worth and value in God's eyes. As members of the body of Christ, we are called to live in community, bearing one another's burdens and building each other up in love (Galatians 6:2; Ephesians 4:16).

Truth and Love

Christ embodied both truth and love. He never shied away from speaking hard truths, but He always did so out of love. This balance is challenging to maintain, especially in a culture that often prioritizes one over the other. As followers of Christ, we are called to speak the truth in love (Ephesians 4:15), standing firm in our beliefs while also showing compassion and understanding to others. Truth without love can be harsh and condemning, while love without truth can be sentimental and permissive. But when truth and love are held together, they reflect the heart of Christ, who is full of grace and truth (John 1:14).

Trust and Surrender

Finally, if Christ is King, we are called to trust and surrender to His will. This can be difficult, especially when we face trials and suffering. But as we see in the story of Job, God's ways are higher than ours, and we may not always understand His plans. Yet we are called to trust in His goodness and faithfulness, knowing that He is in control and that His plans are for our ultimate good (Proverbs 3:5-6). Surrendering to Christ's kingship means letting go of our own agendas and trusting that His will is perfect, even when it leads us through difficult or uncertain times.

If Christ rose from the dead, then He is indeed the King of Kings and Lord of Lords. His resurrection validates His identity and teachings, giving us a glorious hope and future. This reality calls us to surrender to His authority, live selflessly, build community, speak truth in love, and trust in His wisdom. It is a challenging path, but it is the path to true fulfillment and purpose.

SUMMARY OF KEY POINTS

- If Christ is truly King, His teachings hold ultimate authority.

- His example calls us to live selflessly, build community, and seek truth in love.

- Trusting in Christ's wisdom requires surrender, especially when life's circumstances are challenging.

REFLECTION QUESTIONS

1. How does recognizing Christ as King change your perspective on your daily life?

2. In what areas of your life might you need to surrender more fully to Christ's authority?

ACTION STEP

Identify one area of your life where you struggle to trust in Christ's guidance. Pray for the strength to surrender this area to Him.

CHAPTER 12

A Renewed Humanity

The Gospel is not just an invitation to personal salvation. It is an invitation to a radically transformed identity that breaks down all the walls we have constructed between ourselves. Our world is full of divisions, whether by race, nationality, social status, or political affiliation. But when we come to Christ, these earthly distinctions fade considering our new identity.

In Christ, we are made new (2 Corinthians 5:17). Our identity as Christians transcends anything else that defines us. The Gospel reveals that our primary identity is not rooted in where we come from, the color of our skin, or our political preferences. Instead, it is rooted in the fact that we are sons and daughters of God, united in Christ. This truth is more powerful than any other label we could ever wear.

The Breaking of Divisions

In Galatians 3:28, Paul famously wrote: "There is neither Jew nor Gentile, neither slave nor free, nor is there male and female, for you are all one in Christ Jesus." In that one statement, he shattered the traditional divisions that kept people apart in his world and in ours. The world loves to divide people into categories, to pit one group against another, but the Gospel stands in direct opposition to that way of thinking. In Christ, these divisions lose their power.

Think about it. You have more in common with a fellow Christian living halfway around the world, someone you may never meet in this life, than with a neighbor who shares your nationality, your race, or your political beliefs but does not share your faith. That is how powerful our Gospel identity is. It unites us across all boundaries, not just superficially but deeply, because we share the same Spirit, the same hope, and the same eternal future.

Peter and Paul: A Lesson in Breaking Down Divisions

Even in the early church, divisions threatened to tear apart the unity of believers. In Galatians 2:11-14, Paul recounts the moment he had to confront Peter for refusing to eat with Gentiles when certain Jews were present. Peter's actions reinforced a division that Christ had already broken down. The Gospel of Jesus had demolished the barriers between Jew and Gentile, yet Peter's actions threatened to rebuild them. Paul's rebuke was a reminder that in the kingdom of God, there can be no room for discrimination or division based on ethnic or social lines.

The church in the first century was revolutionary in the way it united people from all walks of life. Jew and Gentile, slave and free, male and female all came together as one family, breaking the social norms of the day. That is the kind of community Christ calls us into today. The Gospel transcends and transforms our cultural differences into something beautiful, creating a new, united humanity.

Jesus and the Samaritan Woman: Defying Cultural Boundaries

Jesus, too, modeled this breaking down of barriers in His ministry. One of the most striking examples comes from John 4, when Jesus spoke to the Samaritan woman at the well. In that one conversation, Jesus broke through multiple barriers that were racial, social, and gender based. Jews and Samaritans did not associate with one another, and men did not typically engage in public conversations with women, let alone one with a questionable reputation. Yet Jesus did not let any of these divisions stop Him. He spoke directly to her, offering her the living water of eternal life. His actions demonstrated that the Gospel would not be bound by the prejudices and limitations of culture.

Like Jesus, we are called to live out this renewed humanity by engaging with those who are different from us, breaking down the walls of prejudice, and reaching out in love to people from all backgrounds. We do not cling to earthly identities; instead, we embrace the reality of who we are in Christ.

A New Family Across the Globe

One of the most profound realities of being in Christ is that we are now part of a new global family. The Gospel calls us into the body of Christ, a body made up of believers from every nation, tribe, and tongue. This new family transcends language, culture, and geography. Revelation 7:9 gives us a glimpse into this future reality: "After this I looked, and there before me was a great multitude that no one could count, from every nation, tribe, people and language, standing before the throne and before the Lamb."

When we embrace the Gospel, we step into a new family that is bigger than anything we have ever known. We now have brothers and sisters in Christ who live in places we have never been, who speak languages we do not understand, and whose cultures may be completely foreign to us. Yet we share the deepest bond imaginable, the bond of faith in Christ. And that bond is more powerful than anything that divides us.

Politics and Identity in Christ

In a world that is increasingly divided along political lines, it is easy to let our political affiliations become a defining part of our identity. But as Christians, we are called to remember that our allegiance to Christ must always come first. Our identity as followers of Jesus is bigger than any political party or ideology. The Gospel transcends politics, calling us to a higher loyalty, to Christ and His kingdom.

This does not mean we avoid political engagement or ignore issues of justice and morality. But it does mean that we approach these things with the understanding that our true citizenship is in heaven (Philippians 3:20). Our hope is not in earthly leaders or systems, but in Christ alone. And as we engage with the world around us, we do so as ambassadors of His kingdom, not as partisans for any earthly agenda.

Unity in the Body of Christ

Ephesians 4:3-6 calls us to "make every effort to keep the unity of the Spirit through the bond of peace. There is one body and one Spirit, just as you were called to one hope when you were called; one Lord, one faith, one baptism; one God and Father of all, who is over all and through all and in all." Unity in the body of Christ is not just an aspiration. It is a command. We are called to work toward unity, even when it is hard because our unity reflects the oneness of God Himself.

In a world that thrives on division, the church is called to be a witness to something radically different. We are to be a community of people who love one another deeply, across all the lines that usually divide. Our unity is a powerful testimony to the world that the Gospel is real and that Jesus is Lord.

SUMMARY OF KEY POINTS

- In Christ, all divisions—whether race, social status, or nationality— are broken down. Our identity in Him is greater than anything that defines us.

- Paul rebuked Peter for refusing to eat with Gentiles, reminding us that in Christ, all are one (Galatians 2:11-14). Jesus' encounter with the Samaritan woman broke racial and social barriers (John 4).

- We are united with Christians around the world, sharing more with a believer from another culture than with a neighbor who does not know Christ.

- Our primary allegiance is to Christ, not to any political party or ideology. As citizens of heaven, we live for a kingdom that transcends earthly divisions.

REFLECTION QUESTIONS

1. How does seeing your identity in Christ as absolute change the way you view divisions in society?

2. Are there areas of your life where earthly identities or affiliations have taken priority over your identity in Christ? How can you refocus on your Gospel identity?

3. How can you work toward greater unity within the body of Christ, both locally and globally?

ACTION STEPS

- This week, make a deliberate effort to connect with a fellow believer from a different background or culture. Listen to their story and discover how Christ has united you despite your differences.

- Set aside time to pray for the global church, asking God to strengthen the bonds of unity across national and cultural lines.

CHAPTER 13

He Chose You

This chapter represents the culmination of years of study, reflection, and personal struggle with one of the most profound mysteries of the Christian faith, the tension between free will and predestination. This is not a truth that came easily to me. I spent years questioning how free will could coexist with God's sovereign choice, and it took deep moments of prayer, study, and humility to reach a place of peace with this beautiful mystery. What I have come to realize is that free will and predestination are not contradictory; they are complementary truths that, together, reveal the depth of God's love and grace.

God's Sovereign Choice: A Beautiful Mystery

The Bible presents an extraordinary picture of God's sovereignty. He chose us before the foundation of the world. Ephesians 1:4-5 declares, "For He chose us in Him before the creation of the world to be holy and blameless in His sight. In love, He predestined us for adoption to sonship through Jesus Christ." This is not a cold theological statement. It is the very heartbeat of the Gospel. God, in His infinite wisdom and grace, set His love upon you, knowing every detail of your life, your strengths, weaknesses, victories, and failures. His choice was not based on anything we did or would do. It was rooted in His eternal will and sovereign grace.

This truth leads to a humbling realization. Left to our own devices, we would not naturally choose God. The human heart, in its fallen state, is inclined to turn away from God. In our sinfulness, we seek self over surrender. Romans 3:11 tells us, "There is no one who understands; there is no one who seeks God." And yet, despite our wayward hearts, God chooses us. His love reaches out to us long before we ever think to turn to Him.

Free Will: The Gift of Choice—Yet We Would not Choose Him

Even though we are given free will, Scripture teaches that, without God's intervention, we would never choose Him on our own. We are spiritually dead in our sins (Ephesians 2:1), and dead people cannot choose life. It is only by God's grace, through the work of the Holy Spirit, that we are brought to life and given the ability to respond to Him.

This is what makes the love of God so profound: He loved us first. 1 John 4:19 reminds us, "We love because He first loved us." Our ability to love God and respond to His invitation does not originate from us. It is a response to the love He has already poured out on us. God, in His mercy, awakens our hearts to His love, enabling us to choose Him.

This reality does not diminish our free will. Instead, it highlights the beauty of God's grace. He does not force us to come to Him; He draws us lovingly. Jesus said, "No one can come to me unless the Father who sent me draws them" (John 6:44). God initiates the relationship, but He does not do so in a way that overrides our humanity. He invites, He calls, and He awakens, and in response, we freely come to Him.

Accepting the Tension

This balance between God's sovereignty and our responsibility to choose Him is a tension I have personally struggled with for years. How can God predestine us, yet we are still called to make a choice? How do free will and predestination fit together in a way that makes sense?

What I have come to realize is that this tension is not something we can fully resolve this side of eternity. And yet, as I have learned to live in the tension, I have found peace in knowing that God's ways are higher than ours (Isaiah 55:9). I no longer see these truths as opposites, but as complementary pieces of a greater truth. God's sovereignty does not negate our free will; it perfects it. By His grace, He empowers us to do what we could never do on our own, respond to His love.

You Were Chosen in Love

The most astonishing truth in all of this is that God's choice is rooted in love. "In love, He predestined us . . ." (Ephesians 1:5). This means that God's choosing of you was not random or detached. It was a deliberate, intentional act of love. Before you ever took your first breath, God knew you, called you by name, and loved you with an everlasting love.

This love is not passive; it is pursuing. God does not simply wait for us to make the first move. Like the shepherd who leaves the ninety-nine to find the one lost sheep, God comes after us (Luke 15:4-7). He chases us down with His grace, not because we have earned it but because He has chosen us out of His boundless love.

Living in the Confidence of Being Chosen

Understanding that you have been chosen by God changes everything. It frees you from striving for worth, approval, or validation from the world. It reminds you that your identity is not based on your performance but on God's unchanging love. You do not have to earn His favor; you simply live in the reality of what He has already done for you.

This truth gives you incredible confidence, not in yourself, but in the One who chose you. It allows you to live boldly knowing that you are part of God's eternal plan. Every moment of your life has been woven into the larger tapestry of His purpose. And no matter what challenges or uncertainties you face, you can rest in the fact that your future is secure in Christ.

A Love That Pursues

The doctrine of predestination does not mean we are passive in our faith journey. Yes, God chose us, but He also calls us to respond. His love is a pursuing love, and His grace continues to work in us every day drawing us closer to Him. Even when we falter, even when we doubt, He is there, inviting us back into His embrace.

This relentless pursuit is at the heart of the Gospel. Jesus came "to seek and to save the lost" (Luke 19:10), and that mission continues today. He seeks us, calls us, and invites us to respond to His grace. If you are reading this and feel distant from God, know that He is calling you even now. You are not forgotten; you are pursued.

Living Out Your Calling

Being chosen by God is not just a theological concept; it is a reality that transforms how you live each day. Ephesians 2:10 tells us that "we are God's handiwork, created in Christ Jesus to do good works, which God prepared in advance for us to do." You are not just saved for eternity. You are called for a purpose here and now.

This calling gives meaning and direction to our lives. We are part of something greater than ourselves—God's grand redemptive plan. Every act of love, every moment of service, every step of faith is part of living out the purpose for which we were created.

As we bring this chapter to a close, I want to leave you with this truth: you are chosen, loved, and called by God. This reality is more than a theological statement. It is the foundation of your identity and purpose. Whether you have been walking with Christ for years or are just beginning to explore what it means to follow Him, know that God's love for you is eternal and unchanging.

The tension between free will and predestination may remain a mystery, but we can rest in the knowledge that God's grace is sufficient, and His love never fails. He chose you, not because of what you could offer, but because of His infinite love. And in that love, He has given you the freedom to choose Him.

So today, I invite you to respond to His call. If you have never accepted Christ, know that He stands ready to welcome you into His family. And if you are already a follower of Christ, let this be a moment of recommitment, remembering that you are chosen for a purpose. Live boldly, love deeply, and trust in the One who called you by name.

SUMMARY OF KEY POINTS

- **You were chosen by God before the foundation of the world. His love is proactive, and without His intervention, we would not choose Him.**

- **We love because He first loved us. Our response to God is only possible because He initiated the relationship through His grace.**

- God's relentless pursuit continues. His love seeks us, even when we stray, and calls us into a deeper relationship with Him.

- Living in the confidence of being chosen frees us from striving and allows us to walk in the purpose God has for us.

REFLECTION QUESTIONS

1. How does knowing that God chose you before the foundation of the world impact your sense of worth?

2. Do you find it difficult to reconcile God's sovereignty with your own free will?

3. How does God's choosing you change the way you view your purpose and identity?

4. When have you experienced God's grace in moments of weakness or doubt?

ACTION STEPS

- Reflect on God's pursuing love. Spend time reading and meditating on 1 John 4:19 and Romans 8 asking God to reveal His love to you in a deeper way.

- Respond to God's invitation. If you have not accepted Christ, take this opportunity to pray and invite Him into your heart. If you already know Him, recommit to living out the purpose for which He has called you.

- Embrace your calling. Identify one way you can live out your purpose this week, whether it is through serving others, sharing the Gospel, or spending time in prayer.

CHAPTER 14

Glorious Future

Our future in Christ is not merely about escaping the hardships of this world or finding personal fulfillment. The greatest blessing of our salvation is an intimate relationship with God—Father, Son, and Holy Spirit which will be perfected in glory. We are invited into the eternal dance of love that has existed from before time began. This is a profound truth: we are not only saved from something, sin, death, and condemnation, but saved for something, intimacy with God. Christ promises eternal life, but he also promises that those who trust in him will know God deeply, intimately, and eternally. Jesus Himself defined eternal life in these terms: "Now this is eternal life: that they know you, the only true God, and Jesus Christ, whom you have sent" (John 17:3, NIV).

Imagine this: We will spend eternity exploring the infinite depths of God's love, wisdom, beauty, and grace. Every moment in the new creation will reveal more of who God is, and our joy in Him will grow endlessly. There will never be a moment of boredom, dissatisfaction, or lack for anything, for we will be fully satisfied in the presence of the Triune God.

The Promise of a New Creation

The Bible paints a stunning picture of what is to come that is more vivid and beautiful than anything we can conceive. In 2 Peter 3:13, we are promised "a new heaven and a new earth, where righteousness dwells." This is not just a hopeful dream for the distant future; it is a guaranteed reality. God is preparing this new creation, and it will be more tangible and real than the world we know now. Every aspect of life as we understand it will be transformed—free from sin, decay, and suffering.

Isaiah 65:17-25 gives us a glimpse into this breathtaking future: "See, I will create new heavens and a new earth. The former things will not be remembered, nor will they come to mind." The heartaches, the struggles, the deep pains of this life will no longer have a hold on us. Instead, our reality will be marked by unending joy and peace. The sound of weeping will be replaced by laughter; the cries of despair will give way to songs of praise.

Revelation 21:4 further deepens this promise: "He will wipe every tear from their eyes. There will be no more death or mourning or crying or pain, for the old order of things has passed away." God Himself will personally wipe away every tear, bringing a complete restoration beyond anything we have experienced. The tears we have cried and the sorrows we have carried will be redeemed in ways we cannot yet imagine. Every loss will be met with restoration, and every wound will be healed by the tender touch of God.

Imagine This New World

Close your eyes and try to picture this: You step into a world unlike anything you have ever known. The air is clean and fresh, as if you are breathing in pure life itself. The sky stretches out in hues of blue more vibrant than anything you have ever seen. The flowers, the trees, the mountains, and the rivers all sing with the glory of God's creation, as if each living thing is alive with joy and purpose.

In this new world, you no longer feel the weariness that comes from the struggles of life. Every part of creation is in perfect harmony with God's design. Imagine walking through streets bathed in light, not the light of the sun, but the glory of God Himself shining in every direction. It is a world where there is no more fear, no more violence, no more injustice. Instead, there is perfect peace, Shalom, which touches every corner of existence.

What is more, there is no trace of sickness or disease. No more cancer, no more panic attacks, no more heartbreak from loss. As Romans 8:21 tells us, creation itself will be "liberated from its bondage to decay and brought into the freedom and glory of the children of God." This is not just a fresh start. It is a complete transformation of everything we know.

Resurrected Bodies: A Glorious Transformation

One of the most profound aspects of our future hope is the promise of resurrected bodies. 1 Corinthians 15:42-44 describes this transformation in vivid terms: "So will it be with the resurrection of the dead. The body that is sown is perishable, it is raised imperishable; it is sown in dishonor, it is raised in glory; it is sown in weakness, it is raised in power." Our current bodies, frail and prone to sickness and decay, will be transformed into glorious, powerful bodies perfectly suited for eternity with God.

Imagine waking up in a body that no longer aches, no longer tires, and is no longer subject to death. The diseases that plagued us, the injuries that limited us, the fatigue that weighed us down will be gone. Every part of us will radiate with the health and vitality that comes from being made whole in Christ. Isaiah 40:31 tells us, "But those who hope in the Lord will renew their strength. They will soar on wings like eagles; they will run and not grow weary; they will walk and not be faint."

But it is not just about physical restoration. Our entire being—body, mind, and spirit—will be made new. 1 John 3:2 promises us: "Dear friends, now we are children of God, and what we will be has not yet been made known. But we know that when Christ appears, we shall be like him, for we shall see him as he is." We will be made like Christ, free from the effects of sin, filled with His righteousness and holiness.

Living in Perfect Community

Not only will our bodies be transformed, but our relationships will be completely healed and restored. Revelation 21:3 declares, "Now the dwelling of God is with men, and he will live with them. They will be his people, and God himself will be with them and be their God." For the first time, we will experience life in perfect communion with God and with one another. All the divisions and conflicts that plague our relationships today, whether through misunderstanding, jealousy, or pride, will be gone.

Imagine what it would be like to live in a community where everyone is known and loved perfectly, no more gossip, no more fear of being misunderstood or rejected. Every person will live in harmony with one another, reflecting the unity of the Trinity itself. Ephesians 2:14 tells us that Christ "has destroyed the barrier, the dividing wall of hostility." In the new creation, all those walls will be gone.

Purpose and Creativity in the New Creation

In this new creation, our purpose will not diminish. It will flourish in ways we can barely grasp. God created us as image-bearers, endowed with creativity, talents, and the ability to cultivate and build. In eternity, these gifts will be fully expressed. Revelation 22:3 says that the servants of God will serve Him, and this service will be full of joy and purpose. Work, as we know it, will be transformed from toil into a creative act of worship.

Imagine using your God-given talents without the frustration of failure or fatigue. Every artist, musician, craftsman, and architect will create beauty that reflects the glory of God. Every gardener will cultivate the earth with ease and joy, growing bountiful harvests that celebrate the abundance of God's provision. Your creativity will no longer be stifled by fear, insecurity, or comparison but will flow freely as an act of love and worship to the Creator.

Colossians 3:23 reminds us, "Whatever you do, work at it with all your heart, as working for the Lord, not for human masters." In eternity, all our work will be directly for the glory of God and the good of His people.

Eternal Joy and Peace

Psalm 16:11 says, "You make known to me the path of life; you will fill me with joy in your presence, with eternal pleasures at your right hand." The joy we will experience in eternity is beyond what we can imagine. It is not temporary or dependent on circumstances. It is the deep, abiding joy that comes from being fully known and fully loved by God. Every moment will be filled with His presence, and every desire will be fulfilled in Him.

This joy will be matched by peace. Isaiah 25:8 tells us that God will "swallow up death forever. The Sovereign Lord will wipe away the tears from all faces." There will be no more conflict, no more anxiety, no more fear. Every breath will be filled with the peace of God, the peace that surpasses all understanding (Philippians 4:7).

Imagine waking up every day with no worries, no stress, and no fear. Instead, your heart is filled with perfect contentment, resting in the knowledge that everything is exactly as it should be, in the presence of your Creator.

Our Role as Heirs with Christ

As children of God, we are more than just recipients of His grace. We are heirs with Christ. Romans 8:17 reminds us that if we share in His sufferings, we will also share in His glory. We not only receive the reward of eternal life, but we will also participate in the rule and reign of Christ over the new creation.

Think about this incredible reality: we will reign with Christ, not as passive spectators but as active participants in His kingdom. Every decision, every act of leadership, will reflect His perfect wisdom and love. 2 Timothy 2:12 says, "If we endure, we will also reign with him." This promise gives our current lives profound meaning and direction, knowing that everything we do now is preparing us for an eternal role in God's kingdom.

The glorious future that awaits us is more than we could ever dream. It is a future where we will dwell in the presence of God with resurrected bodies, perfect community, eternal joy, and purpose-filled creativity. This hope is not just a distant dream. It is a reality that shapes how we live today.

Let this vision of the new creation fill your heart with hope and inspire you to live boldly for Christ, knowing that your future is secure in Him.

SUMMARY OF KEY POINTS

- **Eternal life in Christ is about entering into intimate, everlasting communion with God, not just escaping earthly hardships. It is about knowing and experiencing God deeply.**

- Scripture promises a new heaven and earth where sin, pain, and suffering no longer exist. Every tear will be wiped away, and joy and peace will prevail.

- Our frail, mortal bodies will be transformed into powerful, imperishable bodies, free from sickness and decay, and perfectly suited for eternity.

- The new creation will be marked by perfect relationships, with no barriers or conflicts as we live in harmony with God and each other.

- Our God-given talents and creativity will find their fullest expression in eternity. Work will be a joyful act of worship free from the frustrations of this life.

- The joy and peace we will experience in God's presence are beyond what we can imagine—complete contentment, free from worry and fear.

- As children of God, we are not just saved but called to reign with Christ in His eternal kingdom, participating in His rule over the new creation.

REFLECTION QUESTIONS

1. How does the promise of a glorious future with Christ influence your present life?

2. In what ways can you live more boldly knowing your future is secure?

ACTION STEP

- Spend time this week meditating on the promises of Scripture (Revelation 21:1-5, 1 Corinthians 15:42-44, Romans 8:18-21) regarding our future. Let this eternal perspective shape how you approach your relationships, your work, and your faith.

CONCLUSION

Firm Foundation for Disruption

As we reach the end of this journey together, I want to extend my deepest gratitude for walking through these pages with me. In a world that is rapidly changing and is filled with incredible advancements and unprecedented disruptions, you have taken the time to explore what it means to find your identity and purpose in Christ. Whether you embarked on this journey with a heart full of questions, seeking clarity in your faith, or simply longing for a deeper understanding of God's love amidst the chaos, I pray these reflections have opened a new way of seeing. One that reveals more clearly who we are, why we are here, and how we can stand firm in this unique time in history.

In this book, we have delved into profound themes of faith, identity, grace, and purpose navigating through the complexities of a world marked by technological advancements, division, and dehumanization. We have seen how our worth is not defined by what we accomplish or how others perceive us but by what Christ has already accomplished for us. We have confronted personal barriers like the desire for approval, validation, control, and security recognizing how they limit our ability to truly serve and love others.

We have explored the foundations of our faith, examining evidence for divine design, the truth of the resurrection, the fulfillment of biblical prophecies, and addressing the problem of suffering. We have delved into the true essence of the Gospel, contrasting it with worldly misconceptions, and discussed how embracing our identity in Christ transforms our daily lives and interactions.

This journey was never meant to simply impart knowledge. It has always been an invitation to experience the fullness of life in Christ and to become a steady presence in a world that desperately needs hope, love, and truth.

A Call to Reflect and Engage

As we conclude, I invite you to reflect deeply on the truths we have uncovered. The challenges of our time: division, isolation, the rise of "Cancel Culture," and the temptation to retreat into echo chambers are real. Yet we are called to be agents of change, to build meaningful relationships, to speak truth in love, to serve sacrificially, to engage graciously, and to stand firm without following the loudest voices or latest trends.

The most important question remains: *How will you live out your identity and purpose in Christ in this disrupted world?*

Our journey does not end here; it continues every day as we seek to know God more intimately and live out our purpose with joy and courage. Whether you have followed Christ for many years or are just beginning to understand the depth of His love, the invitation is always open. Christ calls us to trust Him more deeply by surrendering our lives into His hands which includes:

our fears, desires for control, and need for validation, and to walk in the fullness of His grace.

If you feel God stirring in your heart, if you sense His call to respond to His love and to be a beacon of hope in a chaotic world, do not wait. Christ welcomes you as you are, with your questions, doubts, fears, and failures. He offers a firm foundation amid the shifting sands, a steadfast anchor in the storm.

And if you have been following Christ for a while, this is an opportunity for renewal. Let this be a reminder of the incredible love that has saved you and the divine purpose for which you were called. You are not merely surviving in this life. You are called to thrive, to reflect Christ's love in tangible ways, and to live out His mission with passion and purpose in a world that desperately needs it. As you move forward, carry with you the truth that you are deeply known and deeply loved by the One who created you.

A Moment of Prayer

I invite you now to join me in a final prayer, a prayer that reflects the heart of this journey and asks God to guide our steps as we move forward in this disrupted world.

Heavenly Father,

We stand in awe of Your unchanging love in a world of constant change. Thank You for the gift of calling us Your children, for giving us a new identity and purpose in Your kingdom. Help us to live out that purpose with courage, joy, and compassion, serving and loving others even amid chaos. Remove the barriers within us—the desires for approval, validation, control, and security—that hinder us from fully embracing Your call. Draw us ever closer to Your heart, and may our lives be a reflection of Your grace and truth to those around us. We surrender ourselves—our hearts, our fears,

*our dreams, and our futures—into Your hands, trusting that
Your plans for us are perfect. Empower us to be steady anchors
in this disrupted world, pointing others to You. In the name
of Jesus Christ, our Savior, Amen.*

Moving Forward with Purpose and Grace

While we may have reached the final page, the real journey is only
beginning. As you continue forward, I encourage you to live in
the truth of who you are in Christ: loved, chosen, forgiven, and
called. Your identity in Him is secure, and your purpose is clear.
Embrace it with confidence knowing that God walks beside you,
empowering you with His Spirit and filling you with His grace.

The path ahead will not always be easy. There will be challenges,
doubts, and moments of uncertainty and struggle. But as we have
discovered, we are not called to figure it all out or to carry the
weight of the world on our own. We are called to trust, to surrender, and to walk by faith knowing that our God is faithful to
complete the good work He has begun in us.

The truths we have explored, about our identity, purpose, and
the grace of God, will continue to shape your life beyond these
pages. Let them ground you, inspire you, and lead you into a
deeper relationship with the God who loves you more than you
can comprehend.

As you navigate this disrupted world, remember that you
have a unique opportunity to reflect God's glory to those around
you. By overcoming personal barriers and standing firm in your
faith, you can build meaningful relationships, engage graciously,
and serve sacrificially. You can be the steady presence that this new
era so desperately needs.

As you go from here, remember: You are not alone. The God
who calls you is with you, and His promises are true. He will
guide you, strengthen you, and fill your life with meaning and

joy. Keep seeking Him, keep trusting Him, and keep walking in the beauty of His grace.

Thank you for being part of this journey. I pray that as you continue forward, you will grow ever deeper in the grace and knowledge of our Lord Jesus Christ. May His peace surround you, and may His purpose guide you in all that you do.

Acknowledgments

First and foremost, I want to thank my wife, *Jacqueline*. From the very beginning of this journey she supported me wholeheartedly, never hesitating, even when she knew this endeavor would take more time, energy, and resources than we might ever see returned. Her faith and willingness to follow God's leading, even at personal cost, have been my anchor. I am profoundly grateful for her partnership, support, and unwavering belief in my calling to write this book.

Thank you to my daughter, *Joseline*, for her support and encouragement on this journey. My prayer is she doesn't have to learn as many of these lessons the hard way, as I did and that she rests in her identity, value, and worth in Christ.

Thank you to my friend, *Tim Sansbury*, for always being willing to debate deep theological concepts. Our research and conversations strengthened my understanding as I wrestled with key messages in the book.

A special thank you to *Karen Gray* for walking alongside me as I worked out ideas and concepts. Her willingness to brainstorm, listen, and ask tough questions helped solidify the core themes of this book. Her steady input was a constant reminder that this effort goes beyond the page, it is a calling to serve others.

I also want to express my deep appreciation to *Roy Milton*, my dad, who encouraged me from day one. Reading multiple drafts, offering constructive feedback and encouragement.

To the many friends and family members who invested their time in reading early versions and providing candid feedback: thank you. Your thoughtful critiques, suggestions, and affirmations have shaped this book into something far better than I could have created alone. Your willingness to journey with me through the writing process has been invaluable, and I am humbled by your generosity.

Finally, my gratitude goes to every person, named and unnamed, who has offered a kind word, a prayer, or a moment of encouragement along the way. Together, we have walked in obedience to a prompt that transcends mere words on paper. It is my hope that this book will, in turn, encourage and bless many others, just as your support and love have blessed me.

Endnotes

Introduction

Keller, Tim. *Counterfeit Gods: The Empty Promises of Money, Sex, and Power, and the Only Hope That Matters.* New York: Penguin Books, 2009.

Lewis, C. S. *Mere Christianity.* London: Geoffrey Bles, 1952.

"Deepfake Detection: Challenges and Advances." *Nature Communications,* 2021.

Part 1 - Identity and Purpose

Chapter 1 - Chaos vs Design

Camus, Albert. *The Myth of Sisyphus.* Translated by Justin O'Brien. New York: Vintage International, 1991.

Lewis, C. S. *The Abolition of Man.* Oxford: Oxford University Press, 1943.

Chapter 2 - Identity

Keller, Tim. *Counterfeit Gods: The Empty Promises of Money, Sex, and Power, and the Only Hope that Matters.* New York: Dutton, 2009.

Chapter 3 - Glorious Purpose

Keller, Tim. *Counterfeit Gods: The Empty Promises of Money, Sex, and Power, and the Only Hope that Matters.* New York: Dutton, 2009.

Keller, Tim. *Every Good Endeavor: Connecting Your Work to God's Work.* New York: Dutton, 2012.

Lewis, C. S. *Mere Christianity.* London: Geoffrey Bles, 1952.

Marvel Studios. *Loki.* Directed by Kate Herron, created by Michael Waldron, Disney+, 2021.

Part 2 - God Revealed

Chapter 4 - God Revealed in the Resurrection of Christ

Keller, Tim. *The Reason for God: Belief in an Age of Skepticism.* New York: Dutton, 2008.

Lewis, C. S. *Mere Christianity.* London: Geoffrey Bles, 1952.

Wright, N. T. *The Resurrection of the Son of God.* Minneapolis: Fortress Press, 200

Chapter 5 - God Revealed in the Bible

Keller, Tim. *The Reason for God: Belief in an Age of Skepticism.* New York: Dutton, 2008.

Wright, N. T. *Jesus and the Victory of God.* Minneapolis: Fortress Press, 1996.

Lewis, C. S. *Mere Christianity.* London: Geoffrey Bles, 1952.

Chapter 6 - The Good News

Hugo, Victor. *Les Misérables.* New York: Signet Classics, 1987.

Keller, Tim. *The Prodigal God: Recovering the Heart of the Christian Faith.* New York: Dutton, 2008.

Lewis, C. S. *Mere Christianity.* London: Geoffrey Bles, 1952.

Part 3 - Application

Chapter 7 - Understanding Suffering and God's Control

Keller, Tim. *Walking with God through Pain and Suffering*. New York: Dutton, 2013.

Lewis, C. S. *The Problem of Pain*. London: Geoffrey Bles, 1940.

Marvel Studios. *Loki*. Directed by Kate Herron, created by Michael Waldron, Disney+, 2021.

Chapter 8 - Humble Confidence

Keller, Tim. *The Reason for God: Belief in an Age of Skepticism*. New York: Dutton, 2008.

Lewis, C. S. *Mere Christianity*. London: Geoffrey Bles, 1952.

Chapter 9 - The End of Self-Righteousness

Keller, Tim. *The Prodigal God: Recovering the Heart of the Christian Faith*. New York: Dutton, 2008.

Lewis, C. S. *Mere Christianity*. London: Geoffrey Bles, 1952.

Chan, Francis. *Crazy Love: Overwhelmed by a Relentless God*. Colorado Springs: David C. Cook, 2008.

Hugo, Victor. *Les Misérables*. Paris: A. Lacroix, Verboeckhoven & Cie., 1862

Chapter 10 - Living in Freedom

The Matrix – Directed by Lana and Lilly Wachowski, released by Warner Bros. Pictures, 1999.

Chinese Bamboo Tree analogy – Commonly used motivational metaphor for unseen growth before visible progress. Origin in Chinese horticultural traditions (no specific publication cited; widely referenced in motivational literature).

Part 4 - Implications

Chapter 11 - Christ is King

Avengers: Endgame – Directed by Anthony and Joe Russo, released by Marvel Studios, 2019.

Chapter 12 - A Renewed Humanity

Wright, N.T. (2013). *Paul and the Faithfulness of God*. Fortress Press.

Keller, T. (2012). *Center Church: Doing Balanced, Gospel-Centered Ministry in Your City*. Zondervan.

Stott, J.R.W. (1986). *The Cross of Christ*. InterVarsity Press.

Chapter 13 - He Chose You

Packer, J. I. *Evangelism and the Sovereignty of God*. InterVarsity Press, 2001.

Packer, J. I. *Knowing God*. InterVarsity Press, 1993.

Piper, John. *Desiring God: Meditations of a Christian Hedonist*. Multnomah Publishers, 2011.

Sproul, R. C. *Chosen by God*. Tyndale House Publishers, 1994.

Chapter 14 - Glorious Future

Lewis, C. S. *The Great Divorce*. HarperOne, 2015.

Piper, John. *Future Grace: The Purifying Power of the Promises of God*. Multnomah Publishers, 2012.

Wright, N. T. *Surprised by Hope: Rethinking Heaven, the Resurrection, and the Mission of the Church*. HarperOne, 2008.

Conclusion

Keller, Timothy. *The Reason for God: Belief in an Age of Skepticism*. Dutton, 2008.

Lewis, C. S. *Mere Christianity*. HarperOne, 2001.

Piper, John. *Don't Waste Your Life.* Crossway, 2003.

Wright, N. T. *Simply Christian: Why Christianity Makes Sense.* HarperOne, 2006.

Tozer, A. W. *The Pursuit of God.* Christian Publications, 1948.

Additional Resources

OpenAI. "ChatGPT." OpenAI, 2023. https://www.openai.com.

About the Author

Joseph L Milton is a husband, father, and lifelong learner who is passionate about helping others discover their true identity and purpose in Christ. With a background in leadership, strategy, and consulting, he has witnessed firsthand how technological advances and cultural shifts can unsettle even the strongest foundations of faith. Through his writing, Joe seeks to offer thoughtful, practical insights that equip believers to navigate a rapidly changing world without losing sight of the timeless truth of God's love. Joe strives to build authentic connections, engage in meaningful conversations, and share the ever-relevant power of the Gospel.

He can be reached at josephlmiltonjr@gmail.com